HOUSES FOR SMALL SPACES

EDITED BY GARY TAKLE

With text by:

Emma Peacock

Jade de Souza

Corey Thomas

CONTENTS

HOXTON HOUSE

DAVID MIKHAIL
Architect

10-11 Clerkenwell Green,
London EC1R 0DP

Phone: +44 207 608 1505

www.davidmikhail.com

ABOUT THE ARCHITECT

Working closely with clients to make exceptional custom-designed homes, each project produced by David Mikhail Architects is unique, tailored to brief and location.

Established in 1992 and based in Clerkenwell Green, London, their work has achieved numerous awards and has been widely published both in the United Kingdom and abroad. The projects represent excellent value for their clients and are often created within tight budgetary constraints.

In 2005, he co-founded a sister practice to David Mikhail Architects – Riches Hawley Mikhail, which specializes in public projects.

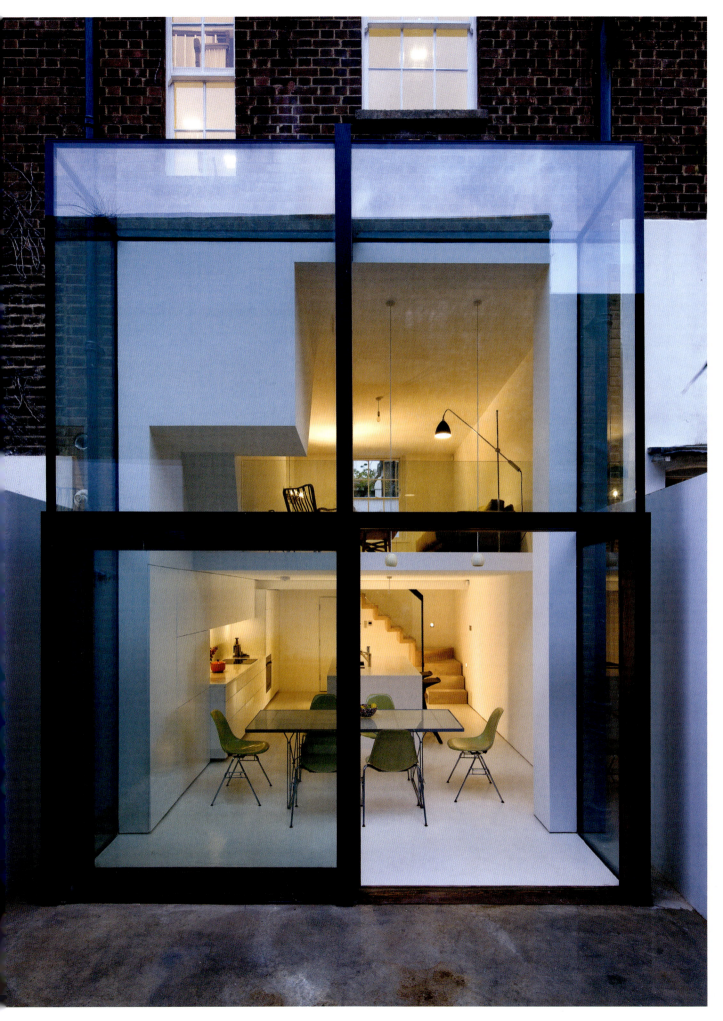

A complicated arrangement of pokey rooms stacked over several stories comprised the Hoxton House, a typical 19th Century terrace home in England. The kitchen was located underground in a semi-basement under a ceiling height of only two metres. A small rear courtyard was part of the home's saving grace, affording the owners some much desired outdoor space on their tight urban lot. Access to this space, however, was via a half landing off a cramped service staircase down to the kitchen.

Desiring a new kitchen and dining area that permitted relaxation and conversation whilst food was being prepared, as well as an elegant space to entertain friends and family, the young couple who own the home employed David Mikhail, confident that his ingenuity would provide them with a perfect outcome.

Mikhail successfully transformed this disordered home into one that suited the couple's modern condition, and did so in a way that was modest in scale but grand in architectural order.

The new rooms have essentially been carved from the original terrace house, permitting the rear courtyard to remain and the rooms to engage actively with it. An extension of only one metre allows for the new above-ground kitchen, dining area, sitting area and bathroom. By slotting the new spaces more or less within the envelope of the existing property, the potential for engagement with the courtyard has been unlocked.

The bespoke double-story cruciform façade has been engineered from high quality Douglas fir and structurally bonded double-glazing. The double height does much to challenge the homes original aesthetic whilst at the same time lightly and effortlessly blending with it.

A bright white kitchen reflects the light brought in through extensive glazing as does the white concrete floor, offset by natural materials and the warm brick hues of the small courtyard. A void extends over the dining area, affording the space a sense of openness once thought impossible in such a small property. Above the kitchen, a sitting room – contained inside a practically invisible glass balustrade – is a lovely space to recline and relax overlooking the rear courtyard.

Chic and stylish, these interior spaces are decorated with pieces that make a modern reference to eras past while at the same time celebrating the contemporary nature of its makeover. Warm tones of green and orange articulate a stand-out décor, perfectly complementing what is a unique and impressive remodel.

Photography by Tim Crocker.

Basement

Ground

TERRACE HOUSE

This refurbishment and extension to an early 20th Century house on a narrow block provides the residents with more space and new rooms in a contemporary, modular re-imagination of the original property. The result is a charmingly modern, restored home that has provided the clients with a free, dynamic interior space and a fresh, engaging exterior.

This small extension, slipped between two larger terrace properties, used to be a library adjoining the house. This reconfiguration represents an architectural triumph for the designers, highlighting the advantages of the site and turning an unattractive and no longer functional space into an aspect of the home that adds value and ultimately exceeds the customer's expectations of what could be achieved.

The refurbishment included the construction of a double garage and photography studio in matte black, adding two new functional spaces to the property. The home and the studio/garage bookend the narrow property, creating a haven-like garden between these contrasting buildings.

The interior is pervaded by a sense of ingenuity, with custom spaces either discreet or featured depending on their use. The laundry room is unobtrusive and tastefully hidden, but the gallery and study area overlooks the kitchen and garden room, creating a dialogue between the two spaces and uniting them in a central feature of the house.

The glazed garden room – far from being an afterthought – is a re-evaluation of interior verses exterior space, drawing the garden into the kitchen and through the open house, allowing a flood of light into all the spaces.

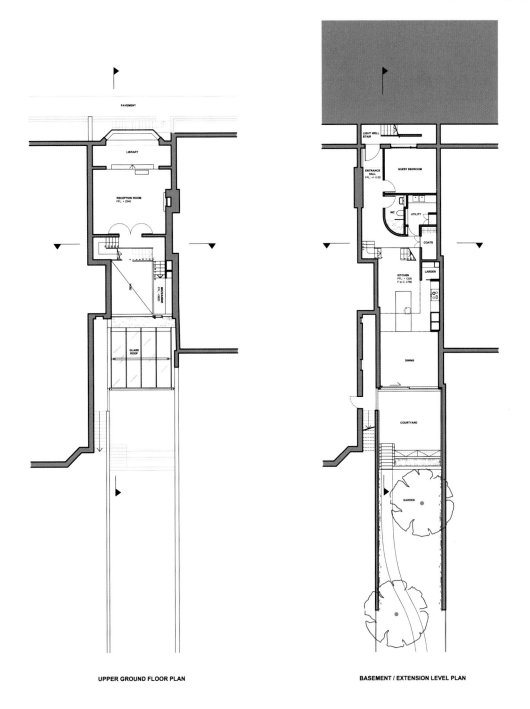

UPPER GROUND FLOOR PLAN

BASEMENT / EXTENSION LEVEL PLAN

A sophisticated palette enhances the bright, fresh feeling of the house. Light grey and white, broken only by coffee coloured timber floors afford this home a sense of unparalleled modernity and elegance.

Photography by Julian Cornish Trestrail

David Mikhail DAVID MIKHAIL ARCHITECTS   10-11 Clerkenwell Green, London EC1R 0DP, UK   Phone: +44 207 608 1505

www.davidmikhail.com

PIER ONE

LUCIANO BOLOGNA
Designer

40-42 Errol Street,
North Melbourne VIC 3051 AUS

Phone: +61 3 9329 0282

www.2bs.net.au

ABOUT THE DESIGNER

From an early age, Luciano has been interested in the design of houses. Growing up , Harry Seidler was his architectural idol and he was inspired by the world of Santiago Calatrava. Luciano has over 20 years experience in the design and construction industry.

With a strong background in engineering combined with his instinctive flair for design, he explores and pushes the boundaries on what is possible with built form. Luciano's style tends towards the quirky, bold and dynamic, encompassing movement in a solid physical form.

The Project: Unique and eye-catching, this exceptional design by 2bScene reflects the mood of the waterfront. The owners approached designer Luciano Bologna with a desire for something different, a quirky design that was also minimalist and captured the waterfront views.

Given that the adjacent sites to the east and west would soon be occupied, it was imperative that as much natural light and ventilation be brought in through the north and south elevations, as well as through the roof – an interesting objective of the four storey home.

The design breaks away from the horizontal layering of levels by fronting the streetscape with a double height window. The artistic feature of rock-like patterns articulated by the window 'frames' is cased by a protruding edge designed to focus outward views and permit natural light and warmth to flood the living area, at the same time blocking harsh westerly sunlight from overheating the space.

Similarly maximizing the natural light brought into the home, skylights work together with a clever stairway – encased in glass to permit light to filter down through the levels of the home. Thus internally, the home feel spacious despite the narrow site upon which it is built.

The interior of the home is minimalistic letting the light shadows and reflections decorate the spaces. The kitchen is defined by the lowered black ceiling protruding out from a wall of reflective black cabinetry. A striking marble island bench does its part to establish the monochromatic palette exhibited throughout the remainder of the minimally furnished house.

Glass balustrades and the angles of the walls reflect the sinuosity of the stairs – as well as bouncing the light from the skylight of the third level. The stairs therefore become the light core of the house. Steel rods act as balustrades for the void, permitting that natural light to filter down into the entryway and acting as a visual connection between the two floors. The double height ceiling above the living room has a crow's nest observation platform above, reflective of the marina environment.

Backing onto a canal and a private jetty, the rear of the house expresses its four levels unusually through varying protrusions of the external balconies to each floor, a design feature geared towards the framing of views. Despite the small 240m2 parallelogram shaped infill site, the house makes a grand statement from both the street and the water, giving little away of its surprisingly spacious inside.

Photography by David Yeow

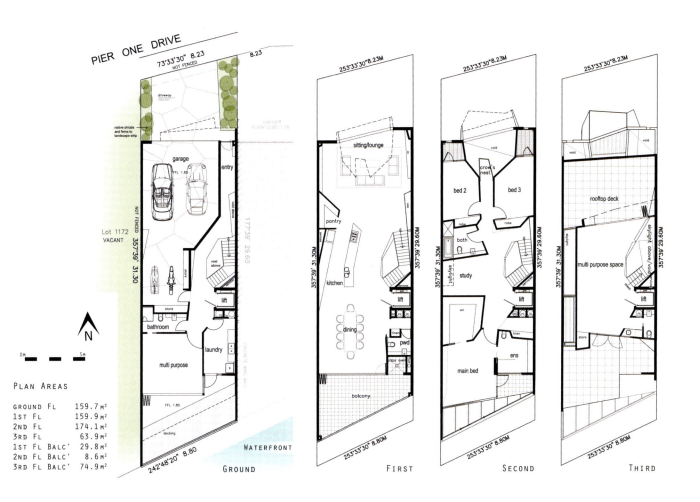

PIER ONE DRIVE

73°33'30" 8.23   8.23
NOT FENCED

driveway

native shrubs
and ferns to
landscape strip

GARAGE
FLOOR LEVEL 1.78

garage
FFL 1.85

entry

void above

Lot 1172
VACANT

357°39' 31.30   NOT FENCED

177°39' 29.60   CONCRETE RETNG WALL

void
above

lift

store

store

bathroom

laundry

multi purpose

FFL 1.85

decking

242°48'20" 8.80

WATERFRONT

GROUND

N

0m — — — 5m

PLAN AREAS

GROUND FL   159.7 m²
1ST FL   159.9 m²
2ND FL   174.1 m²
3RD FL   63.9 m²
1ST FL BALC'   29.8 m²
2ND FL BALC'   8.6 m²
3RD FL BALC'   74.9 m²

253°33'30"8.23M

sitting/lounge

pantry

kitchen

357°39' 31.30M   357°39' 29.60M

lift

dining

linen

pwd

pizza oven

balcony

253°33'30" 8.80M

FIRST

253°33'30"8.23M

void

crow's
nest

bed 2   bed 3

robe   robe

both

357°39' 31.30M   study   357°39' 29.60M

lift

wir

linen

main bed

ens

253°33'30" 8.80M

SECOND

253°33'30"8.23M

void   void

rooftop deck

357°39' 31.30M   multi purpose space   skylight above void   357°39' 29.60M

lift

store

253°33'30" 8.80M

THIRD

uciano Bologna - 2BSCENE DESIGN   40-42 Errol Street, North Melbourne VIC 3051 AUS   Phone: +61 3 9329 0282

ww.2bs.net.au

WRITER'S STUDIO

**WENDY EVANS JOSEPH
& CHRIS COOPER**
Archtitects

500 Park Avenue, Suite 16E
New York NY 10022 USA

Phone: +1 212 935 3392

www.cooperjosephstudio.com

ABOUT THE ARCHITECTS

Cooper Joseph Studio, formerly Wendy Evans Joseph Architecture, is a creative collaboration between Chris Cooper and Wendy Evans Joseph – building upon a portfolio that began in 1996.

Wendy Evans Joseph began her career at the offices of Pei Cobb Freed & Partners. She holds a BA summa cum laude from the University of Pennsylvania, as well as a Master in Architecture with 'Distinction' from Harvard University Graduate School of Design. Additionally, she is a Fellow of the American Academy in Rome and the American Institute of Architects.

Chris Cooper has a skilled design sensibility stemming from the knowledge of large-scale practice blended with small-scale client-centered sensitivity. He joined the firm after a decade at SOM, New York where he ran an integrated design group. At Cooper Joseph Studio, the practice has flourished with his expertise and reductive modernist aesthetic.

The Project: Immersed in woodlands, this distinctive studio is a personal retreat stripped back to absolute simplicity. Referencing the surroundings, the single room focuses on the natural, dappled light and nearby trees. This small cottage is an escape from reality, a place for a busy scientist to get away from his family to work, read and listen to music.

The design is abstract and sculptural in form, using shape, texture and clean lines to strike against the chaotic strokes of nature. This is contrasted by the use of traditional, sustainable and locally sourced materials. Minimalist detailing and glass-to-glass panels at open corners challenge the simplicity of the 'box' shape.

The exterior siding is cedar, stained matte black. It is used as flat panels and smaller dimension slats. Shadows from the deep woods catch the slats and enliven the

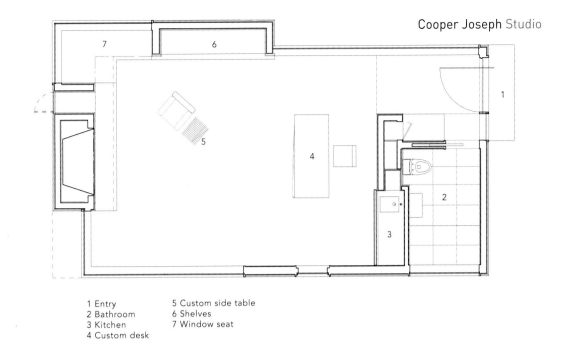

1 Entry
2 Bathroom
3 Kitchen
4 Custom desk
5 Custom side table
6 Shelves
7 Window seat

elevations with a subtle play of light across the exterior. Custom designed copper rain scuppers and wall caps elegantly accent the dark surfaces.

This elegant darkness is a theme continued throughout the studio. Harsh winters in the region necessitate a thematic warmth, and this is achieved through a central fireplace, the heart of the studio. It serves as a visual center, lending support to the structural frame and anchoring the asymmetrical composition of two cantilevered corners.

The fireplace hearth is formed of local cleft-face black slate, and this is also used on the bathroom walls and floors. The interior is finished in walnut, including the highly polished floor, the large sliding doors, the slatted walls and even the bathroom sink. The sink is custom designed, with a grooved surface bringing water to a recessed drain. This ensures that no piping is visible.

The desk, a formal counterpoint to the predominantly orthogonal design, is a series of folded triangular planes, a smooth surface that complements the walls. A low reading table has the same type of sculptural design, but is slatted to reference the wall décor while creating the illusion of planes.

This small studio is a serene, sophisticated, modern cave that provides a haven away from home, hidden and isolated in the woods.

Photography by Elliott Kaufman Photography

Cooper Joseph Studio   500 Park Avenue, Suite 16E, New York NY 10022 USA   Phone: +1 212 935 3392

www.cooperjosephstudio.com

THE BACHELOR PAD

GARY CATT
Architect

49a Station Street
Malvern VIC 3144 AUS

Phone: +61 3 9509 4650

www.cattarchitects.com

CATT Architects have made residential architecture their passion for over 25 years. Gary Catt was originally a refugee from the commercial architectural world who wanted to focus on individual 'lifestyle architecture' rather than formulistic $/sq. architecture.

Within the specialty of designing 'houses', the projects have ranged from inner city in-fills to suburban residences, out to extensive country estates. The practice works both in Australia and the USA.

As the website shows, the projects extend from the small lot boutique to prestigious homes to urban villages. The focus on client support and project control has established CATT Architects as one of a hand full of recognized top-end designers in the residential field. Their work has been featured in national and international magazines and books, and continues to be acknowledged with industry awards.

The Project: This project presented a huge challenge. On an extremely small triangular allotment there was a heritage overlay, a two-storey height limit and a spatial brief that seemed to require well over 100% site use plus the inclusion of external entertainment spaces.

The house was to be both a refuge for the owner as well as a place to entertain in, with an open plan living space focused around the pool and spa area. Along with that, it had to have a spacious garage to fit the owner's Aston Martin.

Built boundary to boundary, the building is a triangular box. The only setbacks are at the front for a minimal garden and on the north side for sun access. The north facing side – adjacent to the laneway – literally peels open via a full, stackable glass panel wall. Beyond this is a two-storey void with a glass balustraded walkway that traverses the space to access the three first floor bedrooms.

All rooms over both levels directly connect with the central void that below creates a two-storey indoor/outdoor entertainment space. A falling water feature provides constant, gentle noise to block out traffic from the street.

Geared toward fun and entertainment, this house caters to the needs of a sports-mad bachelor who entertains frequently. The style is open and airy, and spaces flow inside to outside seamlessly. Swimming is a priority, and most of the limited outdoor space is dedicated to a pool. However, the effortless transition between inside and out sees the interior take the place of an al fresco area. The adjacent kitchen is a fun space, full of gadgets and ideal for a man who loves to cook.

The principal feature corner of the property was necessarily taken up by the garage, as there were problems with access in any other position. Rather than apologizing for or trying to hide the garage, it has become a feature itself. A huge panel of folded seam copper cladding above the 'graffiti' line draws and reflects the golden late afternoon sun. The front of the house sets back with a garden at the front to echo adjacent cottages. The picket fences prevalent in the street are simulated by cantilevered steel flats protruding from a concrete plinth.

Inside, 'art' walls are set at angles to protect artwork from direct sunlight. Upstairs, the en suite is elevated so that it is possible to watch the soccer on the bedroom TV whilst cocooned within the egg-shaped stone bath.

Photographer: Lupco Veljanovski

Details of Size:

Site Area: 232m²

Ground Floor: 140m²

First Floor: 140m²

Total: 280m² (30SQ)

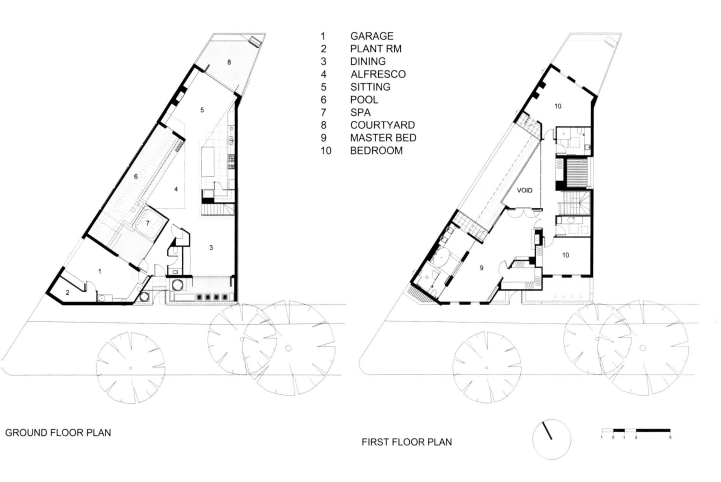

1	GARAGE
2	PLANT RM
3	DINING
4	ALFRESCO
5	SITTING
6	POOL
7	SPA
8	COURTYARD
9	MASTER BED
10	BEDROOM

GROUND FLOOR PLAN

FIRST FLOOR PLAN

Gary Catt - CATT Architects   49a Station Street Malvern VIC 3144 AUS   Phone: +61 3 9509 4650

www.cattarchitects.com

SMALL HOUSE

DOMENIC ALVARO
Architect

Level 10, 17 York Street,
Sydney NSW 2000 AUS

Phone: +61 2 9249 2500

www.woodsbagot.com

ABOUT THE ARCHITECT

Recognised as a new emerging voice in Australian architecture, Domenic is a designer who insists on the uniqueness of every architectural experience and the importance of architecture within its particular context.

As lead designer in the Sydney Woods Bagot studio, Domenic continues to build upon 15 comprehensive years of experience within numerous international architectural offices by overseeing the design and realisation of many varied-scale, award-winning architectural projects.

At present, Domenic is currently engaged in a number of new typology-pushing residential developments, and has recently completed his own residence, entitled 'Small House', located in Sydney. 'Small House' is an exemplar in urban consolidation and an innovative case study in precast concrete living space construction.

On a site so small that it could fit into the garage of your typical suburban home, 'Small House' is a compact, vertically expressed dwelling that adds intrigue and interest to the urban fabric of Surry Hills in New South Wales.

An exercise in urban consolidation, 'Small House' assigns multiple uses to single spaces, allowing for flexibility in the future. Vertical zoning sees the ground floor comprised of utility and storage areas, the first floor sleeping, bathing and storage areas, the second floor living and the third floor containing cooking, eating and entertaining spaces. Topping this stack is a rooftop garden terrace - a luxury on the small urban site. A small study space is included on the roof, with operable panel sliding doors extending the room outward. A series of open stairs connect all the spaces and allows light to filter through the internal rooms.

The philosophy of this project was to pre-plan it in its entirety to ensure that as many components could be pre-made in the factory as possible. The structure, built entirely from high quality precast concrete, was fabricated off-site and erected over a mere four day period.

'Small House' is not only an example of exceptional architectural features complimented by meticulously planned interior design, it addresses the issue of urban sprawl. It is a unique project that presents an affordable way to stylishly live in the inner city, opening up practically every unused backyard, shed or parking space to development and challenging collective ideas of how much space really is needed for comfortable living.

Photography by Trevor Mein

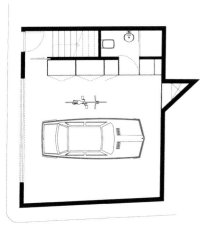

Ground Level

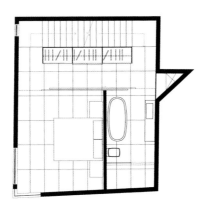

First Level

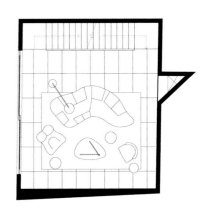

Second Level

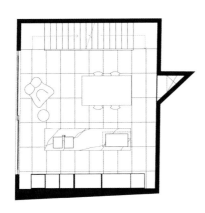

Third Level

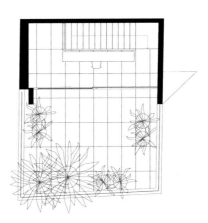

Roof

Domenic Alvaro - WOODS BAGOT   Level 10, 17 York Street, Sydney NSW 2000 AUS   Phone: +61 2 9249 2500

www.woodsbagot.com

STRELEIN WAREHOUSE

IAN MOORE
Architect

5/151 Foveux Street,
Surry Hills NSW 2010 AUS

Phone: +61 2 8354 1887

www.ianmoorearchitects.com

ABOUT THE ARCHITECT

Born in New Zealand, Ian has previously worked with Beca Carter Hollings and Ferner in Auckland as well as Ove Arup and Partners in London.

Ian Moore Architects was established in 1990 and was in partnership with Tina Engelen as Engelen Moore between 1996 and 2005. Ian has taught at the University of Technology, Sydney, Sydney University, University of New South Wales and the Sydney Institute of Technology and has received a Master of Architecture degree, from RMIT University, Melbourne in October 2000.

The practice has won numerous national and international awards; including the apartment building Altair, which won both 'Best Building in the Australasia/Oceania region' and 'Best Housing Scheme in the World' at the World Architecture Awards in 2002, Berlin; in 2006 a Dedalo Minosse International Prize Commendation and an International Architecture Award, awarded by The Chicago Athenaeum: Museum of Architecture + Design, both for the 138 Barcom Avenue Apartments. In 2011 Strelein Warehouse won numerous awards including an International Architecture Award awarded by the Chicago Athenaeum: Museum of Architecture + Design and the inaugural AZ Award for Interiors: Residential.

The work of the practice includes single residential projects, multi-unit residential developments, mixed use developments, large scale urban renewal projects, as well as commercial, retail and residential interiors, with projects currently in Sydney, Broome and Auckland.

The Project: Once a humble grocery warehouse, this remarkable residential conversion by Ian Moore Architects re-instills in the market a growing trend for warehouse transformations. Epitomizing urban chic, this exciting property showcases a palette predominant of blacks and whites, with sleek fixtures and fittings that emphasize quality and understated style.

From the street, the unassuming brick façade says more about the character and history of this property and its surrounds than any new home could. With a compact footprint of only 150m², the existing building occupies the entire site, with no external space.

Avoiding the typical 'cellular' style of smaller, high-rise homes, maintenance of large, light-filled rooms was paramount to the design. As such, this dictated the composition of the home, which includes one bedroom, and adjoining living, dining and entertainment areas.

Few problems arose from local authorities regarding the retention of certain features of the 115 year old building, however it was decided that the existing timber windows and doors were not original and consequently allowed for the reinstatement of authentic window openings and the insertion of new steel-framed windows. The lower level comprises of the main 'living' areas, with the kitchen, dining and lounge rooms all positioned close together, facilitating a healthy family environment.

The upper level of the home is essentially one large open space, with a black box bathroom at its centre. Here, black aluminium clad walls climb only to the height of the original building, where an additional set of clerestory windows brings extra height and light without detracting from the single-volume characteristics of the room. Making use of louvers, this feature also enables cross flow ventilation.

Of particular importance to this building is the joinery, internal door systems and the external paneling to the bathroom. These are what define the home as curious, unique and of premium quality. In the bathroom, brilliant Corian sheet fills the walls and floor, while custom designed vanity basins have been moulded using the same materials. A wall of mirrors has also been employed here to visually extend the sense of space and reflect light around the room.

Encapsulating the design with its renewable philosophy, the floors in adjoining spaces are clad in natural rubber tiles – both recyclable and environmentally friendly, the tiles give a degree of softness underfoot.

Photography by: Iain D. MacKenzie

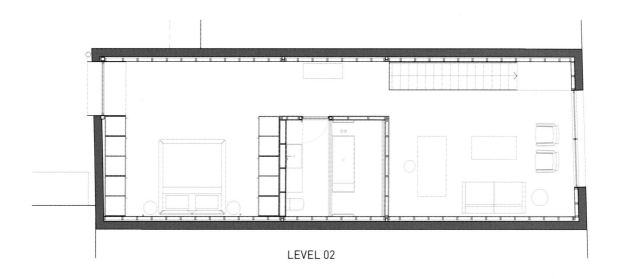

LEVEL 02

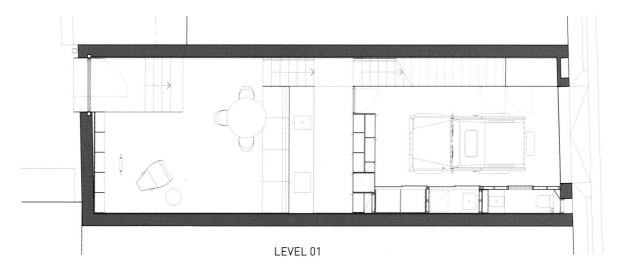

LEVEL 01

Ian Moore - IAN MOORE ARCHITECTS   5/151 Foveux Street, Surry Hills NSW 2010 AUS   Phone: +61 2 8354 1887

www.ianmoorearchitects.com

SLIT HOUSE

ANNA NAKAMURA
Architect

TAIYO JINNO
Architect

Chezmoi Espoir 202 12

Sumizome-Cho Fukakusa

Pushimi-ku, Kyoto 612-0052
Japan

www.eastern.e-arc.jp

ABOUT THE ARCHITECT

Anna Nakamura and Taiyo Jinno founded the Eastern Design Office in Kyoto in 2003. They carefully chose the word 'Eastern' as a describer in their title as a reference to the rising place of the morning star.

Anna Nakamura was born in 1974 in Osaka, Japan and educated at the Faculty of Engineering, Hokkaido University. Taiyo Jinno was born in 1968 in Aichi, and obtained a Master of Architecture from the Graduate School of Science and Technology, Nihon University.

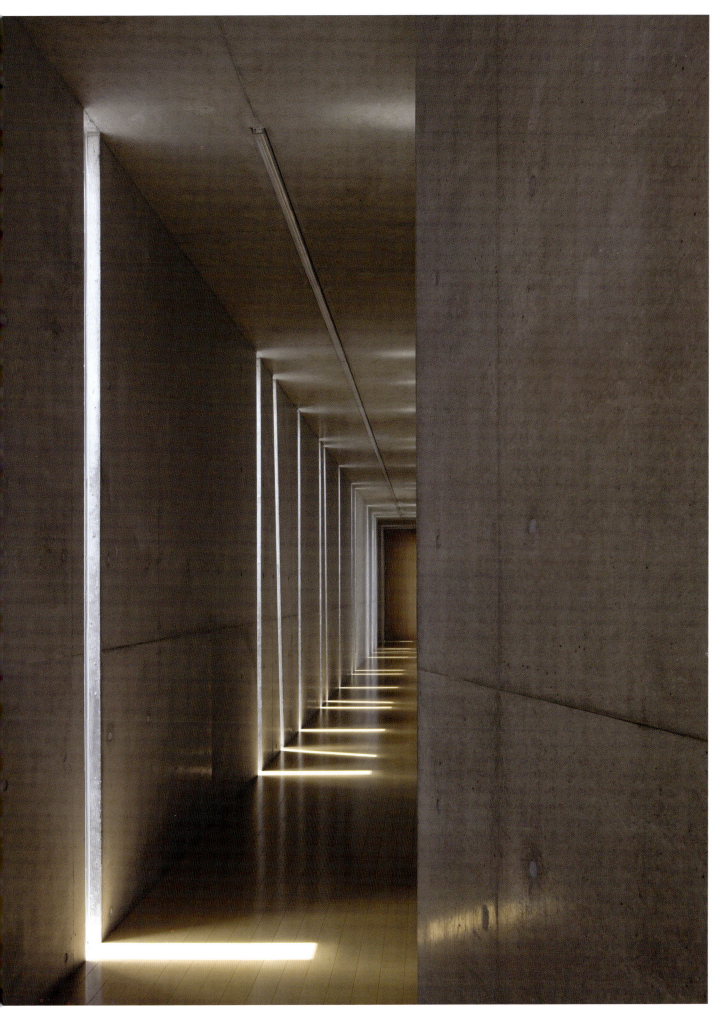

The Project: This narrow, long site presented a unique challenge and was met with a unique response. The form of the house is realized only in the breaks in the wall, the 'slits' or incisions into the extended concrete façade. Deliberately isolating itself from the glass-heavy style of contemporary architecture, this house is a conceptual sculpture. Without a single window, it is distinguished by its outline and abstracted from the surrounding architecture.

The house is situated in a row of private houses in an old city in Japan. The site is 50m deep but only 7.5 m wide, and has two narrow frontages, one to the street and one to a river. The long concrete wall that delineates the property encloses the long, narrow space, and this enclosure is then opened by the slits. The slits – 140mm in width – screen the inner world of the home's tenants from the outside whilst drawing light into the house.

There is a silent ambiance and a poetic clearness offered by the architecture of this house. The promise of an innovative design method offered by the slits is not unrealized in the interior spaces, which are defined by the exterior wall. Though built between two straight lines, there are deliberately juxtaposed walls inside, with curves and unusual room shapes providing a striking, unusual contrast with the sleek, modern sophistication of the exterior.

This monolithic house is not imposing. Instead it is simple, built only using glass and concrete. The attention to light makes it uniquely warm, but without large windows, the atmosphere inside the house is stable and quiet – almost cave-like.

The incisions into the house act like a sort of time-piece, making the house a distinct space depending on the seasons and the time of day.

This house caters to the lifestyle of an elderly woman and provides her with a space filled with soft light and the interesting experience of living in a house of unlikely scale and form.

Photography by Koichi Torimura

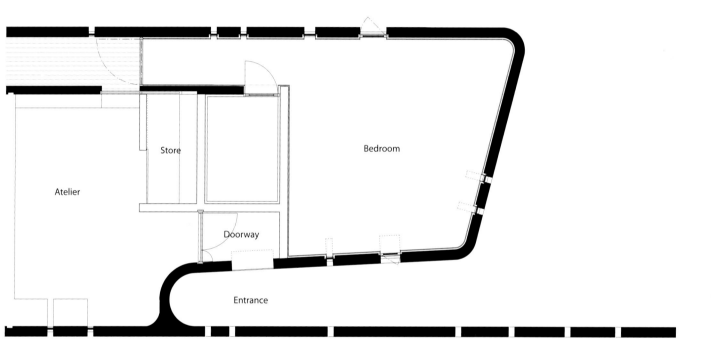

Atelier

Store

Bedroom

Doorway

Entrance

Anna Nakamura and Taiyo Jinno - EASTERN DESIGN OFFICE   Chezmoi Espoir 202 12

Sumizome-Cho Fukakusa Pushimi-ku, Kyoto 12-0052 Japan   www.eastern.e-arc.jp

STRANGE HOUSE

HUGH STRANGE
Architect

210 Evelyn Street
London SE8 5BZ UK

Email: hughstrange@mac.com

www.hughstrange.com

Established in 2011 following the construction of the Strange House – architect Hugh Strange's family home – Hugh Strange Architects is a practice concerned with architecture as a constructive art. Hugh Strange Architects are an intelligent practice, forming specific approaches to environmental and structural situations and challenges.

Hugh Strange studied at Edinburgh University and has worked for a number of design-led practices in London.

Warmth and unobtrusive logic inform the design of this family home. Combining the desire for a low budget house on a constrained site that was environmentally sound and spacious enough for a growing family was a challenge, well met with a design that adheres rigorously to a sensible acknowledgment of the union of materials. The feel of a family home however, comes from the attention to detail, the textural juxtapositions and the careful consideration of the house's geometry that Strange and his team attended to.

Located in London's southeast, it is sited rather inauspiciously in what was once a pub garden. The block is mostly concealed from the nearby street by an existing perimeter wall. From the street the house looks like nothing so much as a warehouse. It is unassuming, a narrow door in the brickwork giving only a glimpse of the elegant family home behind the wall.

Rather than setting the home immediately against the stone perimeter, slim gaps form a narrow path around the property. These slender walkways allow the home to breathe in the small space it is afforded, and enhance the sense of cosiness the space embodies. The old brickwork speaks of the history of the site, and this links a thematic concern of the house – the juxtaposition of materials to create a striking, emotional space.

The foundations of the house comprise two concrete slabs. The old slab is visible around the garden, and the new slab forms a small terrace, extending into the home as a polished concrete floor.

This abundance of concrete could seem cold, but timber furniture, exposed structure and detail afford the interior space an undeniable warmth. The kitchen, cupboards, seating and shelving units in the entry living space sit within recesses formed in the frame, acknowledging the logic and order the house embodies.

Though it is so small – the house itself only 75m2 – high ceilings throughout the property and long rooms make the house feel palatial. With the large sliding door open, the internal house borrows the existing external brick walls, extending the internal space outward and making the house feel even larger. The modest courtyard however, reigns this open feeling in, blocking out the city beyond and creating a private world for the owners.

Photography by David Grandorge

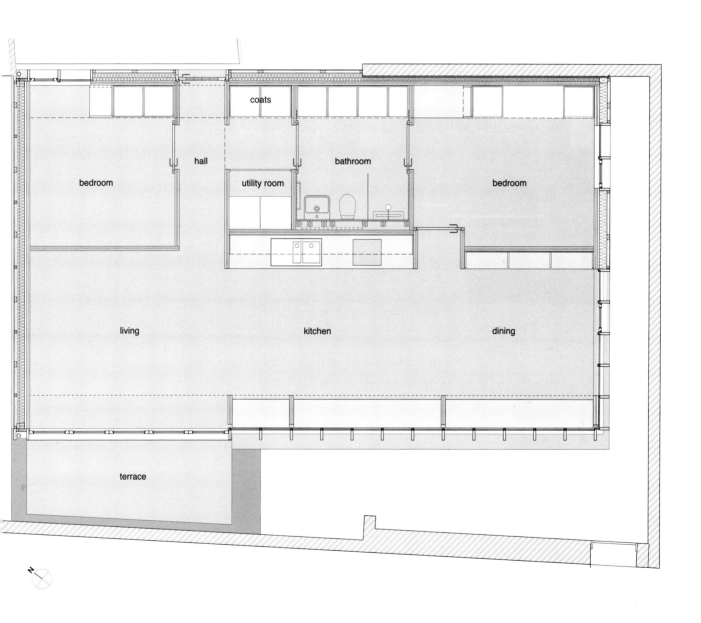

BALACLAVA HOUSE

GREG McNEIL
Designer

MAT WRIGHT
Architect

ABOUT THE DESIGNER

Greg McNeil launched his practice Bios in 2009, his focus to pursue inspirational design for life.

Greg's design journey began after graduating in 1989 and developed through extensive commercial, residential, hospitality, retail and interior design projects while appointed with some of Australia's largest Architectural firms. His extensive experience culminated however in his desire to return to bespoke residential design through Bios.

His inspiration is drawn from his travels to America, Europe and Asia, from where he interprets international style into elegant, sustainable solutions designed for the Australian lifestyle.

Mat Wright is appointed Architect with one of Melbourne's premier architectural practices.

The Project: Though demolished to make way for its exciting new replacement, the dilapidated house that once stood on this slight, urban property lives on through the building form and material of the now standing house. There is a deliberate omission however, of all traditional adornment such as eaves, fascias and fretwork – a decision that satisfied the designers' desires to create a neighbourhood sensitive house with a contemporary sensibility.

Two young designers Greg McNeil and Mat Wright – keen to enter the real estate market but mindful of the challenges faced in this pursuit as individuals – decided in pooling intellectual and financial resources towards their common goal. The result is a modest but extremely sophisticated single storey, detached residence that provided both investors with a stylish and personal place to dwell.

The house has been zoned to provide the two occupants with a private wing that includes bedroom, bathroom, laundry, study and landscaped courtyard. The wings are separated by a U-shaped dining, kitchen and living area that enjoys a northerly aspect and wraps around a central, communal courtyard.

Even with the ample space provided to each inhabitant and the shared living area, the home takes up a mere 140m^2 of the 300m^2 site. The success of the design response lies in its planning and the designing out of the circulation space usually associated with a terrace type allotment. Rather than running a long corridor down one side of the house interior, a timber deck extends its full length. Onto this unconventional passageway, French and bi-folding doors open up every room to deliberate and planned outlooks as well as bringing warm northerly light into each internal space. They aid in the formation of generous volumes and challenge the home's terrace nature.

As well as its pitched roof form, resting quietly amidst the single frontage homes that line the street, external materials similarly blend into the streetscape. Galvanized corrugated roofing and painted timber weatherboard cladding are both economical and sustainable in their compliment to the streetscape.

Like the exterior, the interior is simple but highly considered. A collection of free flowing spaces, few confined by doors but rather segregated via zoning, comprise the internal floor plan. Atop coloured and honed, heated concrete floors floats a minimalistic collection of colours, textures and furnishings expressed in bright whites and soft linens. Lightly furnished lounge and dining rooms flank a long, linear, white kitchen behind which the mirrored splashback gives depth to the narrow allotment.

Combining the owner's love of sensitive, thoughtful architecture and stylish but easy living, this well designed home – conceived and created by the owners themselves, Greg McNeil and Mat Wright – is a showpiece of restraint resulting in radiance.

Photography by Paul Glasser of CT Creative

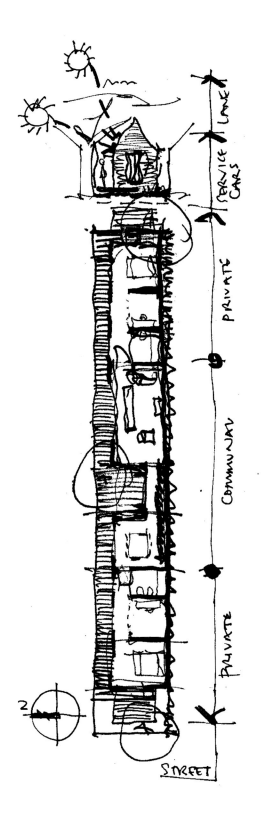

CAMPERDOWN HOUSE 1

SHAUN CARTER
Archtitect

L1/142 Smith Street
Summer Hill NSW 2130 AUS

Phone: +61 2 9799 4472

www.carterwilliamson.com

ABOUT THE ARCHITECT

"Shaun came to architecture the long way round. He'd always wanted to be an architect, but in year ten, a meddlesome careers advisor told him "he'd end up driving taxis" if he pursued his architecture dream. Her comments sent Shaun on a ten-year detour through structural engineering...

Several years after completing his engineering degree, Shaun was working for a building firm when he received a call out of the blue from a friend studying architecture; her lecturer needed someone to drive a bus on an architectural tour around Europe. That night Shaun quit his job, and two weeks later he was in France.

The first days of the trip were a Le Corbusier tour de force; a two night stay at La Tourette, a night at the Unite D'Habitation, but it was when standing in Ronchamp, nearly moved to tears that Shaun realised architecture was calling. That was 15 years ago, since then Shaun has gone on to receive first class honors in his Architecture degree, received the Board of Architects Award in 2000, and has spent 10 years in practice, establishing Carterwilliamson Architects in 2004. He believes architecture has never been more exciting or more fulfilling."

The Project: Whilst this home feels contemporary at first glance, a closer look reveals the building's Victorian roots. Reinterpreted by Carterwilliamson Architects, the compact dimensions of the home fail to limit the innovation displayed and flaunted throughout.

Creating an urban refuge from the hustle and bustle of the city, the house can accommodate a growing family and pets with plenty of space outdoors for play. Efficient use of space has enabled the home to be used to its full potential.

With a site of just 193.4m2, careful planning and effective use of space was imperative to the success of the design. Here, adaptability is key, allowing versatility of floor space depending on the need for use. As such, many of the greatest elements of the home are attributed to the more 'inconspicuous' aspects of the design. These include deep window reveals that double as seating, a wide hallway that also functions as the children's play space, a living room that opens up onto the rear yard, and sliding walls between the kids' rooms to extend their play area.

A tight and efficient floor plan is where this home comes into its own, with a central void above the kitchen and dining rooms introducing a flood of light into the focal point of the home, and promoting a sustainable approach to saving power. Light is provided here after sundown by three sculptural pendant lights acting as another example of versatility being both practical and visually stimulating.

The interior treatment is one of restraint and consideration, with bright, 'retro' furnishings bringing a 70's cool to the modern residence.

An open dialogue was maintained by the architects, builders, clients and local authorities so as to negotiate the design of a contemporary home in a street predominantly filled with Victorian styled homes. It was this dialogue and the design that evolved from it that has led to the local council using this property as an example of good architecture in sensitive heritage areas.

Photography by Brett Boardman

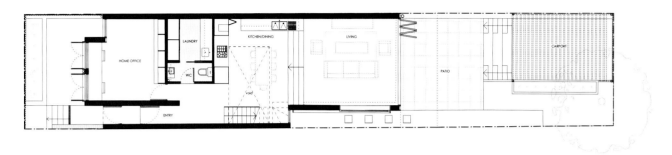

carterwilliamson/camperdown house_1

n plan ground

0   1   2   3m

carterwilliamson/camperdown house_1

n plan level 1

0   1   2   3m

Shaun Carter - CARTERWILLIAMSON ARCHITECTS   L1/142 Smith Street Summer Hill NSW 2130 AUS   Phone: +61 2 9799 4472

www.carterwilliamson.com

THE 100K HOUSE

Interface Studio Architects

1400 N American Street #301
Philadelphia, PA 19122, USA

Phone: +1 215 232 1500

www.is-architects.com

ABOUT THE ARCHITECTS

ISA is an architectural practice based in Philadelphia that serves a diverse range of clients on a number of project types. Their work shares uniting elements – uncompromising commitment to design and research and a pragmatic approach to innovation based on a transparent process of decision making.

Founding Principal of ISA Brian Philips directs the design trajectory of the office. With a degree from the University of Oklahoma and a Master of Architecture from the University of Pennsylvania, he has lectured widely on the impact of telecommunication, affordable housing and the work of ISA. Brian is a lecturer in the Architecture Department at the University of Pennsylvania School of Design where he teaches design studies focused on urban housing.

Principal architect Daryn Edwards is an experienced designer and manager, and a strong advocate for high performance construction, community design and quality urban development. As principal, he manages the daily operations of the studio. He holds a degree from Clemson University and a Master of Architecutre from Iowa State. He has taught at Philadelphia University, and was the former Board Chair of Habitat for Humanity Philadelphia.

The Project: A belief that 'bigger is better' is thriving not only in America but worldwide, and derives from the proliferation of cheap materials, poor quality design and unrealistic economic expectations. ISA believes that small is the new normal. Rather than basing a house's value on its size and marketable features, ISA propose that spatial, material and environmental qualities should be central. This inspired the 100k House, a small, efficient and super-green urban in-fill that provides a sustainable, affordable option for first-time homebuyers.

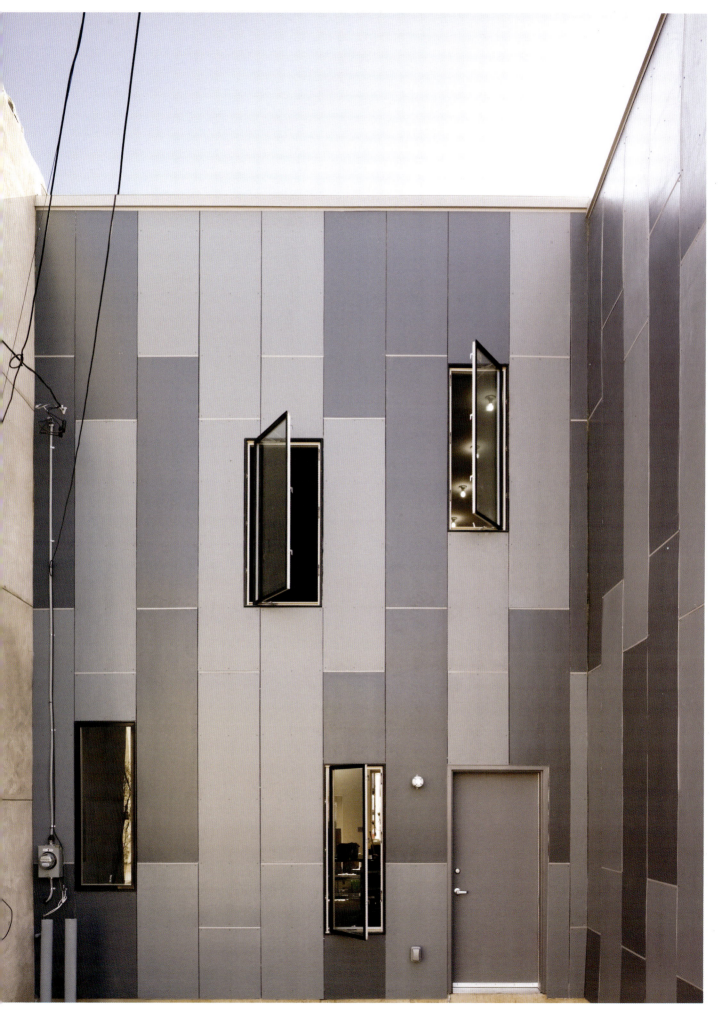

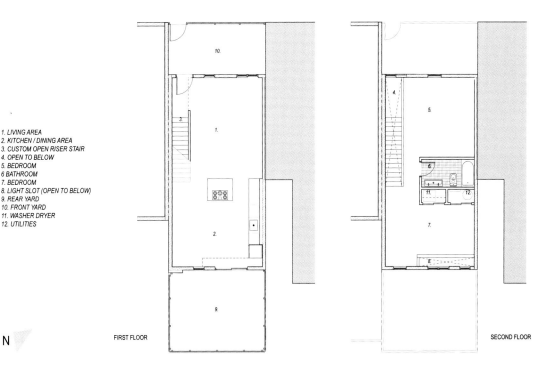

1. LIVING AREA
2. KITCHEN / DINING AREA
3. CUSTOM OPEN RISER STAIR
4. OPEN TO BELOW
5. BEDROOM
6 BATHROOM
7. BEDROOM
8. LIGHT SLOT (OPEN TO BELOW)
9. REAR YARD
10. FRONT YARD
11. WASHER DRYER
12. UTILITIES

N

FIRST FLOOR

SECOND FLOOR

The first 100k House, built in Philadelphia, is efficient and cost effective, exploiting its location for design opportunities. It riffs on simple materials and flush facades, employing texture, pattern and colour as well as low-cost, high-impact treatments to create a striking design that is economical, environmental and affordable.

The interior finishes include plywood, waferboard, exposed concrete and bamboo hardwood. The concrete is cool and provides excellent insulation, but this is contrasted pleasantly with the inclusion of plywood and bamboo, which allow for some aesthetic warmth. The interior design elements are all implemented with the minimalism and sustainability central to the design in mind.

The living spaces are open and flow easily into each other. The kitchen and small living space located downstairs are natural, light filled areas that do not compete with one another in aspect or form. The kitchen, though small, is supremely functional and allows for entertaining and comfortable family dining.

The house employs a passive strategy of heating and cooling focused on a tight, well insulated building envelope rather than a system of heating and cooling. This ensures unique sustainability without compromising the comfort of inhabitants.

Photography by Sam Oberter, except where otherwise stated

Interface Studio Architects   1400 N American Street #301, Philadelphia PA 19122 USA   Phone: +1 215 232 1500

www.is-architects.com

KERET HOUSE

JAKUB SZCZESNY
Archtitect

Belwederska 10/17,
00-762 Warszawa, Poland

Phone: +48 602 316 374

www.centrala.net.pl

Jakub Szczesny is the co-founder of Centrala Designer's Task Force, an interdisciplinary designer cooperative. He has received various prizes and has constructed many buildings including the Bierun Sporthall, Temporary Pavilion of the Museum of Polish Jews, Instituto Cervantes in Warsaw and Stacja Powisle revitalization.

Since 2008 he has worked on both solo and group projects in Poland, Israel, Palestinian Autonomy and Norway. In 2009 he became an expert for the City of Warsaw, participating in an application to the title of European Capital of Culture in 2016 and working on a program for the development of cultural infrastructure of the Polish Capital until 2020.

His interventions in public spaces are oriented towards enhancing environmental conciousness and addressing local social tensions, such as Public Water Purification Island and Synchronicity in Warsaw, Tamaguchi Park in BatYam, Polish Spring in Birzeit, Pchechong in TelAviv and The Lace in Ramallah. Szczesny is also currently working on a concept for a viewing tower in Western Australia's Narrogin.

The Project: This project is the definition of unique, giving new meaning to the design of homes in infill spaces. In the crack between two buildings, forward thinking designer Jakub Szczesny designed an art installation entitled Keret House. This one-of-a-kind project is set to become the narrowest house in Warsaw, if not the world.

Amazingly, the Keret House's interior will vary between 122 and 72 centimeters at the narrowest point. Appropriately, the structure will be a workplace, a heritage created for an outstanding Israeli writer, Etgar Keret. Aside from this, it will also fulfil the function of a studio for invited guests – young creatives and intellectualists from

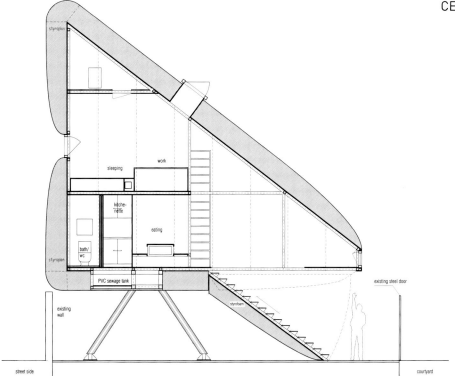

around the world. The residential program is supposed to produce creative work conditions and become a significant platform for world intellectual exchange.

Structurally the house is a simple, tri-dimensional steel frame finished with plywood, insulated sandwich panels and styrofoam covered with concrete cloth painted white. The interior will also be painted entirely in white.

'Living' will place itself on the transformable, remote-controlled, operable stair case that flattens itself when in the 'up' position. A small kitchenette, dining table and toilet fill what remains of the first floor. Acsent up an integrated ladder carries the occupent into a 'private' zone incorporating bed and work area.

The Keret House will be equipped with boat-inspired water and sewage technology that is independant from city systems; the electricity will be delivered by a neighboring building.

Repurposing a derelict space, the 14,5m2 Keret House is a wonder of modern design and a testament to designer Jakub Szczesny's commitment to environmental consciousness. The purpose built strcture will no doubt engage and inspire the creative community and challenge our notions of what a liveable building must be.

Jakub Szczesny - CENTRALA   Belwederska 10/17, 00-762 Warszawa, Poland   Phone: +48 602 316 374

www.centrala.net.pl

BARCODE HOUSE

DAVID JAMESON
Architect

113 South Patrick Street
Alexandria VA 22314 USA

Phone: +1 703 739 3840

www.davidjamesonarchitect.com

ABOUT THE ARCHITECT

A graduate of Virginia Tech, College of Architecture and Urban Studies, David Jameson is an architect of distinction. Having won numerous awards both locally and internationally, his work is uncompromised by the economic shift that has restrained the scope of architecture in recent times.

David Jameson Architect, Jameson's design studio, has been operating for a decade. Embracing the notions of simplicity and the elemental (what he refers to as the 'architecture of distillation') his buildings and renovations address the inconsistency inherent in the production of modernist buildings and renovations within the context of a historical city like Washington DC.

David focuses on deriving a design from the unique pressures offered by each project's site. As such, the spatial logic of each unique home that David Jameson Architects produce is immediately discernible, both from inside and outside. Conceived as a marriage between industrial production and artisanal work, David's innovative designs bridge the gap between these separate worlds, juxtaposing the refined and the raw.

The Project: To the rear of an unassuming row house rests a striking extension. Expressed in glass and steel, the new transparent living space includes a kitchen with entertaining deck, a sitting room and a rooftop deck joined by a new stairwell.

Entitled the Barcode House, steel bars run at various intervals on specifically articulated elements of the design including the deck balustrade, two window panels and across a slight skylight to the living area.

The Barcode House was formed by converting the project's diverse pressures into a unique situational aesthetic. The brittle masonry walls of the existing Washington DC row house dictated that the addition be engineered as a freestanding structure, with the site constraints informing vertically oriented spatial solutions. A stucco circulation tower to one side anchors the living space to the existing row house.

The clients desire for transparent living space generated the opportunity to create an integrated solution for lateral force requirements. Structural steel rods within the glass window wall are aligned with datum lines of the neighbouring building elevations, referencing the surrounding landscape without compromising the progressive design.

The bottom level comprises a kitchen with an unusual square island bench which houses part of the kitchen utility and provides a casual dining area. The shape of the island bench addresses the lack of space, ensuring that the room is full but useable, and that no space is wasted. The adjacent walls bear integrated cabinetry, providing practical storage space and removing the feeling of clutter.

A narrow but adequate flight of stairs ascends to a casual but stylish living area from which one can gaze out over the neighbourhood. The rooftop deck offers an even better vantage point, the perfect place to spend a warm Sunday afternoon with friends.

Surprisingly, with the exception of custom made kitchen cabinets, all the elements of the house including the windows are off-the-shelf products. The ability to avoid making specialised or one-off components adds to the sustainability of the project.

Strong and light at the same time, the addition expresses beauty in it simplicity. Even though the structure itself is simple and the materials off-shelf, the finished product is a polished and appealing extension that brings new life to the old house and new spaces to the delighted owners.

Photography by Paul Warchol Photography

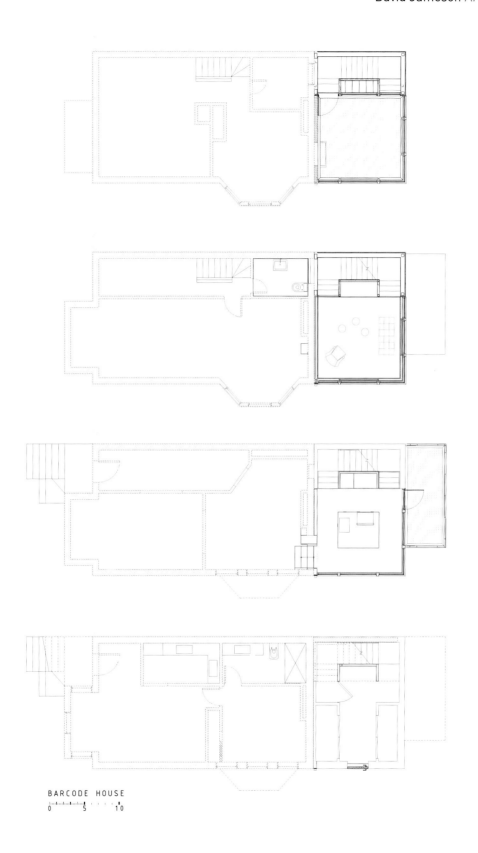

BARCODE HOUSE

0 5 10

David Jameson Architect   113 South Patrick Street, Alexandria VA 22314 USA   Phone: +1 703 739 3840

www.davidjamesonarchitect.com

EASTERN MARKET ROW

Inspired by the image of an illuminated Japanese lantern, this renovation to an existing row house was intended to impart the gift of light to the owner's wife. Comprising a study, a new kitchen and a design studio, this modern, minimalist addition is a study in contrast.

The self-supportive steel frame that cantilevers out of the masonry mass of the existing property serves as a structure for the glass skin of the extension and a visual disparity between the heavy acid-etched panels and the existing brick. The frame unifies the interior as well, providing an intelligent inbuilt shelving solution for the internal spaces.

The presence of the frame is designed to be a tangible presence inside the house, enveloping the kitchen and the second floor study spaces. Vertical partitions deliberately placed throughout the etched window wall allow for the occasional piece of transparent glass to selectively frame views of the sky and trees towards the rear and side of the site.

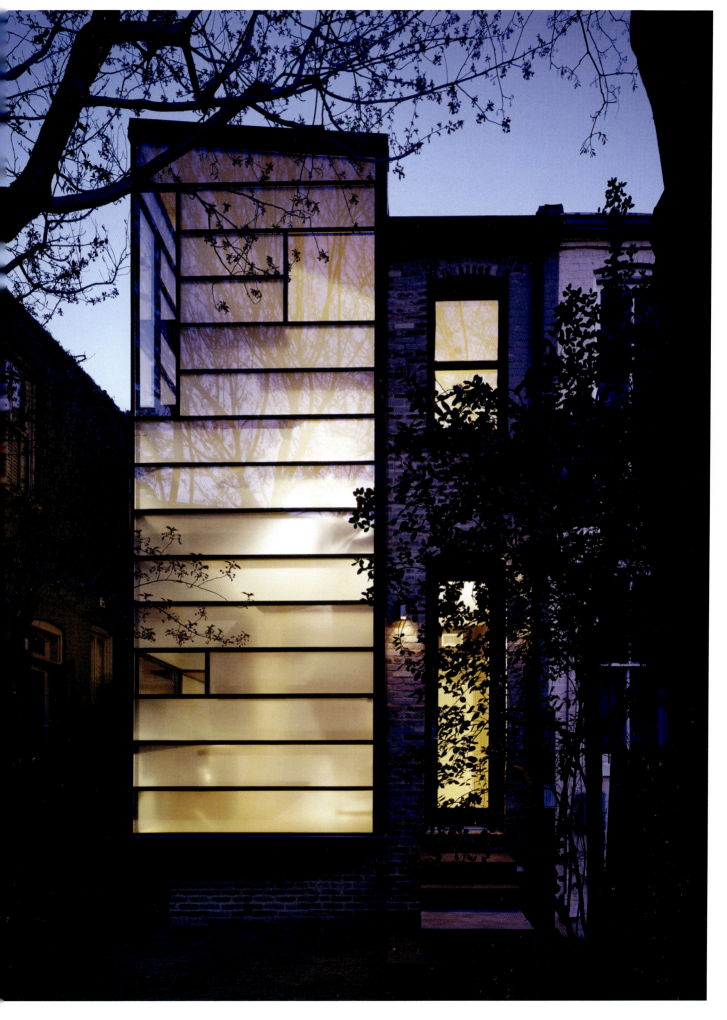

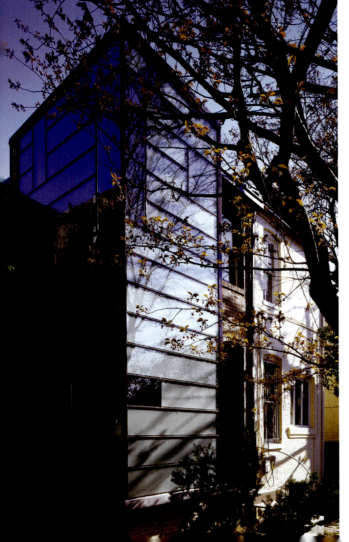

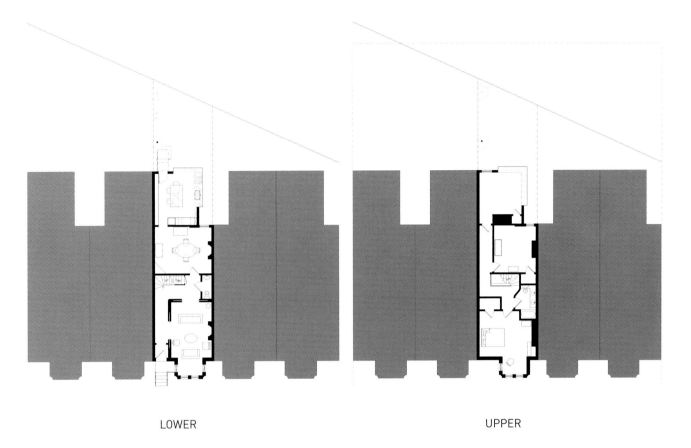

LOWER   UPPER

The interior spaces are dynamic and light-filled, affording the small rooms a spaciousness and a connection with the outdoors. The small-framed windows, created by the placement of clear glass panels throughout, act like hung artwork. The light bamboo timber floor is durable and sustainable, but is aesthetically as beautiful as traditional timber boards.

The cabinetry and additional furniture are all functional and appealing, but minimal in their impact, ensuring that the understated architecture features prominently. Subtle down lights add a warmth to the rooms at night, and give the lamp-like addition an enchanting glow from the exterior.

This award winning addition to the East Market Row House is the first modern residential renovation in the Capital Hill neighbourhood of Washington DC, which required approval from the Capital Hill Historic Preservation review board to be implemented. The application was successful, and the addition seamlessly contrasts with the existing historical home.

Photography by Hoachlander-Davis Photography

David Jameson Architect   113 South Patrick Street, Alexandria VA 22314 USA   Phone: +1 703 739 3840

www.davidjamesonarchitect.com

31WSA - ALBERT PARK

JACKSON FITZROY-KELLY

Design Director

139 Martin Street

Brighton VIC 3186

Phone: +61 3 9596 2200

+61 421 076 036

www.jfkdesign.com.au

ABOUT THE DESIGNER

Jfkdesign landscape|buildings|interiors was established in 2002 and over the past nine years have built a reputation for thoughtful housing design that reflects the needs and lifestyle of the customer, while remaining stylish, contemporary, and sensitive to the surrounding landscape.

Design Director Jackson Fitzroy-Kelly is a landscape architect and building designer who is passionate about the importance of the visual, spatial and environmental considerations in indoor and outdoor spaces. Focusing on sustainability, simplicity and building shape and fabric, Fitzroy-Kelly aims to build houses that suit their owners both now and in ten years time.

Celebrating old and enhancing it with new is a hallmark principle of jfkdesign landscape|buildings|interiors and is something that is always done with respect and restraint.

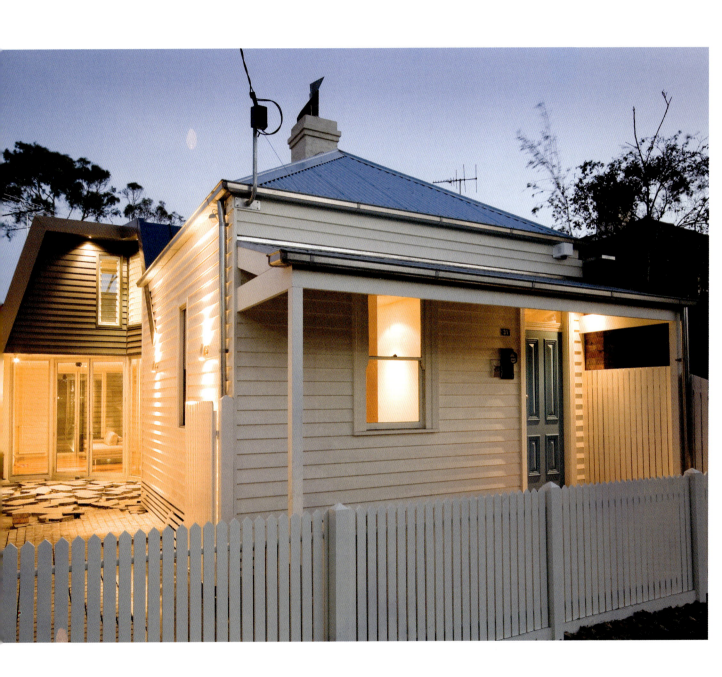

The Project: One of three, two-bedroom worker's cottages lined up by side by side, this period home has been adapted into a spacious family residence that is both mindful of its context and exudes chic contemporary styling. Interior space was made available in a way the original floor plan did not permit, with a slight up and back extension offering the extra room needed to house an additional bedroom, bathroom and new living spaces.

Some large ideas are housed in this cottages limited area. The owner's primary desire was for a home that provided flexible living spaces and smooth transitions between inside and out. They also required additional rooms that did not encroach on their neighbours' privacy and appeased the heritage overlay of the house itself.

The resulting design celebrates and reinstates the original house externally; the verandah, front window, weatherboard cladding and door details all replicate original conditions lost in previous renovations. The restored façade hence connects with the adjacent worker's cottages both stylistically and in material choice. Disguised behind this sensitive façade however lies a contemporary interior perfect for the modern family, with a new living space to the rear and bedrooms upstairs.

Similarly, the new first floor above the rear extension makes a deliberate, fashionable change, the crisp white weatherboard of the ground floor contrasting starkly with the dark addition. The variable angular roof form adds to this juxtaposition whilst complementing the original house and its materiality.

A number of design features are implemented to enhance the sense of space including floor to ceiling doors and varying ceiling heights throughout. Abundant natural light is brought in through skylights above the kitchen, bathroom and staircase, adding to the feeling of openness that departs from the once gloomy atmosphere. These numerous skylights as well as the clever placement of windows and French doors ensure that the sky can be seen from anywhere in the house.

Individual living areas are quite compact, but through the use of differing ceiling heights, two courtyards, abundance of natural light and flexible zoning, each space appears larger than it is.

The living areas wrap around a curved courtyard that can be accessed through the French doors, ensuring adjacent space is used to its full potential. Moments from the beach, the design is perfectly oriented toward catching the sea breeze.

This charming modern design meets the multitude of challenges it faced head on and is better for it. This is an innovative inner-city family home that doesn't compromise the period detail and historical relevance of the façade.

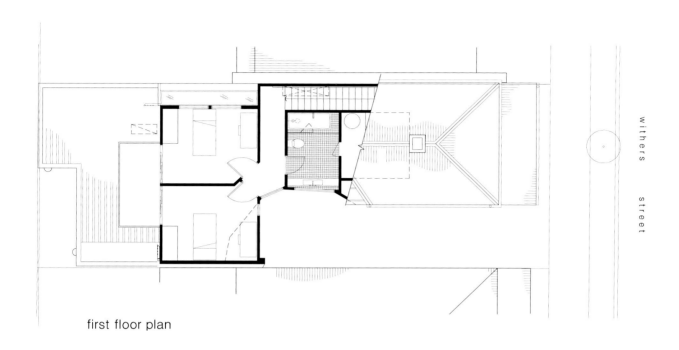

first floor plan

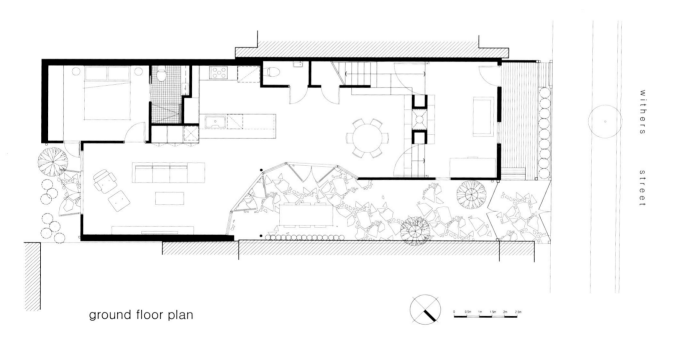

ground floor plan

withers street

withers street

0 0.5m 1m 1.5m 2m 2.5m

YAN LANE

JUSTIN MALLIA
Architect

Phone: +61 409 536 023

ABOUT THE ARCHITECT

Justin Mallia is a young, practicing Melbourne architect with a strong interest in the urban scale, measured with a consideration for the small, detailed and humble in architecture. An interest in the importance of quiet but careful gestures derives from the craft and making aspects of architecture, the expression of the structure and workmanship in a finished project as well as a creative connectedness of design and construction. This sits comfortably with an interest in affordability and the accessibility of good design – that thoughtfully designed objects or buildings do not have to be expensive. This extends to the principle that development projects can achieve financial return through being conceived and driven with a design sensibility.

The Project: Yan Lane is a surprising encounter of tactility, light and tranquility in an otherwise gritty urban setting. Through the creation of an efficient and flexible building that creatively handles the use of space and light with a carefully detailed assemblage of materials, Justin Mallia has crafted an activated, human place from what was previously disused and neglected.

Sandwiched between shop rears and backyard fences was a relatively unwanted site that became home to one of Justin Mallia's greatest architectural achievements - two 150m2 dwellings in 140m2 of space that was previously with no address and no services connection, that was overgrown, littered and inaccessible from a narrow, barely existent right of way.

The two houses present as a single, simple building, contorting themselves in response to the dimensionally tight parameters of the site through a stepped sectional profile.

Each face of the building is assembled with different materials and performs differently to interact between its immediate external context and the internal spaces it encloses. A repetitive structural timber frame is exposed as a consistent organising principle throughout this assemblage, conceptually stitching the façades together and creating a cohesive whole.

Towards the light, tree canopies and residences to the north, the envelope is set back from the structural frame. Wide sliding doors open up the houses to the outdoor space that is created behind layers of extensive customized screens, terraces and plantings. The façades are flexible allowing permeability to be mediated depending on the day.

Material choices and assembly are also geared towards maximum efficiency. For example, rather than cover the structural elements of the building such as the ground floor slab and the plywood flooring that braces the upper floors, these elements are polished and exposed.

Flexible layering of internal and external space, sliding doors, glass, movable screening, terraces and planting results in the creation of a pleasant natural atmosphere in an unexpected dense urban context and is one of the true strengths of the project.

While the building is generally made from inexpensive materials and products, in selected moments more luxurious elements are sparingly but strategically incorporated. Examples include white Carrara marble and a full suite of Blanco appliances and accessories.

Photography by Emma Cross and Paul Cadenhead

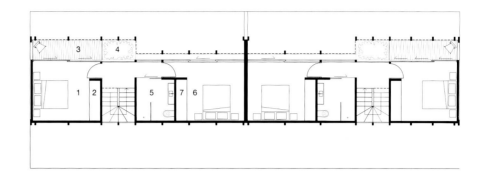

TOP FLOOR PLAN

1. bedroom
2. wardrobe
3. terrace
4. garden
5. bathroom
6. bedroom
7. wardrobe

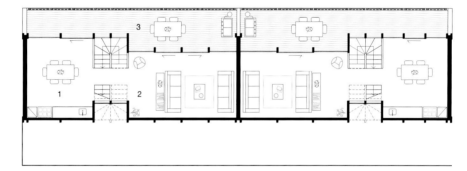

MIDDLE FLOOR PLAN

1. kitchen / dining
2. living room
3. terrace

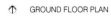
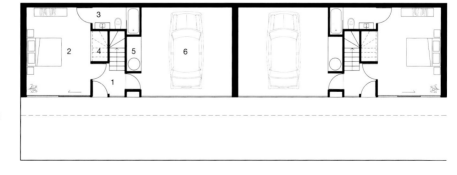

GROUND FLOOR PLAN

1. entry
2. office / studio / 3rd bedroom
3. bathroom
4. store
5. laundry
6. garage

COLOUR BLOCKING

LINDA SIMONS
Architect

ABOUT THE ARCHITECTS

Linda is a graduate of Melbourne University, a Registered Architect and member of the Australian Institute of Architects. She has travelled extensively, including living in Singapore, Tanzania, Munich and Australia, and mixes this wealth of life experience with over fifteen years of practical architectural experience. Proficient in all aspects of architectural services, Linda has worked closely with some of Melbourne's leading interior and landscape architects. Having always directed her own company, now as sole principal, she is excited about future projects which include residential, commercial, hospitality and multi-unit developments.

JUSTIN HOLMAN
Architect

Justin is a graduate of the University of Brighton, East Sussex, where he received an honours degree. He then worked for the internationally recognised firm of Chapman Taylor Architects where he was involved in the concept, design and site implementation of projects ranging from Hotels and Stadia to urban redevelopments. Upon emigrating to Australia in 2001, his experience gained him placement with Denton Corker Marshall and The Buchan Group, where he continued designing and implementing projects both in Australia and overseas. Justin brings his practical and dynamic international experience and his modern, cutting-edge approach to all aspects of his work with LSA.

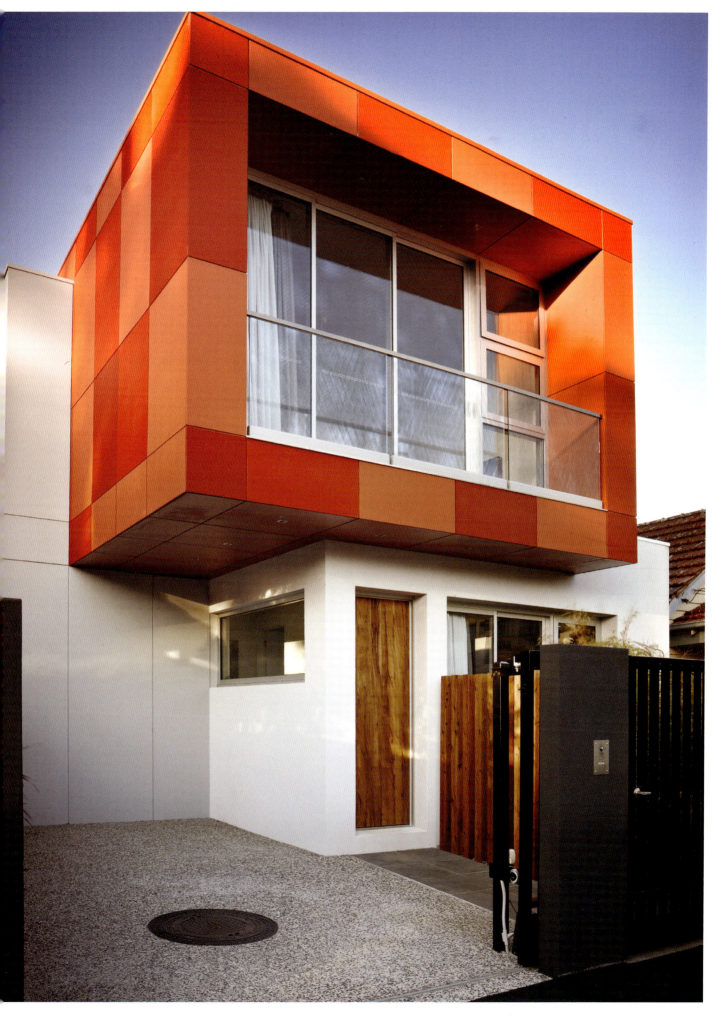

The Project: Taking its inspiration from the rich tones of the owner's contemporary aboriginal painting, this notable house is bold in both colour and form.

It was the goal of Justin Holman and Linda Simons of LSA Architects to provide a house that makes a statement within the eclectic streetscape, capturing one's gaze and holding one's attention upon approach, entry and exploration of the home.

As requested by the property owners, the house blurs the boundaries between interior and exterior. Light-filled spacious internal areas maintain strong connections to the exterior of the structure and the home's multiple courtyards.

The methodology employed to meet these aims included implementing voluminous forms, building to the site perimeter wherever possible, installing glazing to multiple and varied planes, and applying colour to engage the viewer and provide continuity and connection between inside and outside spaces.

From as far away as the end of the street, one can view the orange 'box' that forms the first floor. Upon entry, the white ceiling abruptly gives way to the overhead insertion of this form. Arched glazing either side of the dining area physically separates interior from exterior, yet enables views of the orange-clad ceiling wrapping to form the external walls of the first floor, increasing appreciation of the building as a whole.

The kitchen island bench is similarly finished in gloss orange 2-pac while the dark living room and kitchen joinery are anchored to the room perimeter by virtue of their hue and volume, allowing the internal oranges and external greenery to be the main colour focus. The grey polished concrete of the ground floor and white painted walls provide a subtle yet solid foundation for strategically placed bursts of colour.

Further exploration of colour is found in the master bedroom that features a deep green, referencing the planting of the adjoining south facing courtyard.

Focusing on volume, colour and natural light admission, the home encourages the inhabitants to further its character with the addition of selected furnishings and artworks.

Photography by John Wheatley - UA Creative

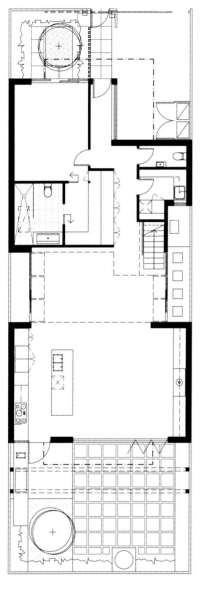

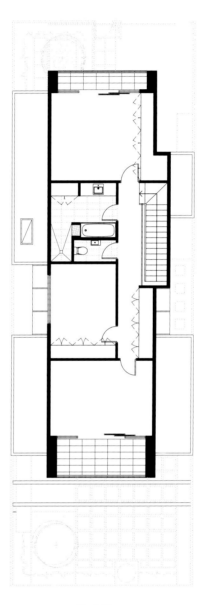

Ground Floor   First Floor

LSA Architects Pty Ltd   27 St. Edmonds Road, Prahran VIC 3181 AUS   Phone: +61 3 9533 8633

www.ls-architects.com.au

THE SHADOW HOUSE

DAVID LIDDICOAT
Architect

SOPHIE GOLDHILL
Architect

Babel Studio One
7 St. Pancras Way
London UK

Phone: +44 020 7380 0977

www.liddicoatgoldhill.com

ABOUT THE ARCHITECT

David Liddicoat studied first at Cambridge University, while Sophie Goldhill trained at The Slade & Bartlett (UCL). David and Sophie met while at the Royal College of Art. Sophie began her career with Sir Norman Foster in London, while David worked for Daniel Libeskind in Berlin.

Experiencing the world of the 'starchitect' – a world of celebrity architects – led David and Sophie to eschew the flimsy formalism of the New Labour years that continue to obsess the profession. Instead, David and Sophie revel in the beauty of practical things and seek to make modest and characterful places to live.

David and Sophie established their practice with the express intention of designing and making houses; the Shadow House is their first completed new build home. They carried out the entire project themselves, from finding the site, through planning, design, construction and manufacture of the fittings, fixtures and furniture.

The Project: The Shadow House is a new build private house in Camden, North London constructed as the primary residence of the architects David Liddicoat and Sophie Goldhill. The house, built inside and out of slim-format Dutch engineering brick with delicate black glaze, is situated on a scrap of land measuring only 38m2 formerly used as a parking garage. The tectonic of the house was driven by its physical and legislative context. The use of Dutch engineering brick, for instance, was informed by the input of Camden Planners, who felt that the house should reflect its tough industrial-era context The result is a robust, monolithic design with an unforgiving monochromatic skin.

In order to give a sense of space to what would otherwise feel like constrained rooms, the designers felt it was important to be able to modulate the section and work with the heights. Different ceiling heights, adjusted by changes in the floor below and by different height roofs produce a range from 3m in the living room to 2.1m in the entrance area. This allowed each space to have its own temperature, sound quality and sense of coziness and airiness. There are certain knots of intensity, where the spatial and functional requirements of the house are tangled up.

One small luxury the designers allowed in their otherwise sparing design was two slabs of bookmatched Staturietto marble, which are used throughout the house as reflective contrast to the brick walls. The design revolves around this play of light and dark; carefully controlled moments of intensity and quiet shadow. The interior spaces are intense, controlled and quiet, creating maximum emotional effect.

The bright first floor bathroom has a huge sheer glass ceiling (which needed to be craned into place) that contrasts with the intense atmosphere of the living spaces. The designers created the sensation of being outside; showering in full sunshine or bathing under the stars.

Spaces are carved playfully into the walls to minimize everyday clutter. The television and cables are concealed behind a black glass wall, the toilet roll has its own marble niche, the washing machine is in a secret cupboard behind the toilet and discrete storage fills every spare corner while the kitchen extract is buried in the brickwork.

The architects, in the interests of turning their house into a space they could comfortably call home, designed their own fittings and furnishings. The Shadow Lamp for example is a granite and laser-cut timber table light that creates a warm ambience in the contrasting house.

The architects now live in the house, and are pleased with the sustainable outcomes achieved by the design. The building performs passively, minimizing the required heating load and eliminating the need for active ventilation. Stable thermal characteristics overcome the challenge of the tempering environment within a building with irregular occupancy.

Resembling a cut face of coal, the striking black is contrasted with sheer, frameless glazing with accents of white staurietto marble, echoing the plaster reveals and porticoes of the surrounding Victorian architecture. Simplicity and functionality combine to frame this house in the great poetry of practical things.

Photography by Tom Gildon & Keith Collie

David Liddicoat & Sophie Goldhill LIDDICOAT & GOLDHILL LLP   Babel Studio One 7 St. Pancras Way London UK

Phone: +44 020 7380 0977   www.liddicoatgoldhill.com

DIAMOND PROJECT

ALEX TERRY
Designer

IVAN TERRY
Designer

ABOUT THE DESIGNER

Terry & Terry Architecture prides itself on its ability to combine innovative architectural theory and practice. The partners, Alexander and Ivan Terry, each have over nineteen years of experience and both offer design concepts and professional production services in architecture.

The partnership has experience with a wide variety of projects, including the design of single and multi residential housing, retail and office space. They have extensive, unique experience with building construction and fabrication that has enabled them to acquire and refine a first-hand knowledge of the relationship between concept, construction and project realization.

Terry & Terry have explored design concepts in urban design in collaborative efforts with other design professionals. In an attempt to improve the built environment, it has engaged in investigations of several concepts in future infrastructures that integrate architecture and planning.

Terry & Terry Architecture aspire to improve the quality of life through design excellence – thus exploring design challenges at all levels with a focus on innovation in response to changing conditions.

The Project: Climbing a narrow, steeply sloping site is a cleverly simple home utilising a minimal palette of materials in the creation of a chic and contemporary structure suitable for family living.

Concrete walls – the raw finish of which has become a prominent interior feature – form the sides of the house and continue back to enclose the backyard. Extending vertically from the garage, through the living area and up over the roof is a third concrete wall that provides a setting for a fireplace and chimney. The use of concrete serves to provide thermal mass for energy efficiency, absorbing heat during the day to keep the interior comfortable on cooler evenings.

Glazing and timber were used to articulate the remainder of the house. The ample use of glass actually allows natural light in and seeks to both capture the views and provide connection to the outdoors.

There is a shared language of simple materials and clean detailing throughout that unifies the interior spaces with the exterior cladding. The aesthetic creates warmth and calmness essential for a family in an urban setting, without distracting from the simple beauty of well-juxtaposed spaces.

Sitting at garden level, the home's main floor houses the common spaces. The living area, blessed with an expansive balcony, takes in the wonderful neighbourhood views. Accessed through a huge sliding door, the balcony is protected by translucent glass, affording the tenants privacy. Back inside, the living room is warmed by an open fireplace cut into the vertical concrete slab running through the centre of the house. A staircase travelling up to the timber lined rooftop deck floats intriguingly behind a translucent glass wall to the living area, providing both a practical and visual feature in the room.

The kitchen space is bright and light-filled. Once again featuring timber, concrete and glass, this is an ideal place to wine and dine with family and friends. Huge sliding doors open the area out to an al fresco terrace set against a lush garden. Amidst the garden sits a small studio that serves as the home office. Since the garden sits within the same concrete wall extending the length of the property, transition between inside and out is blurred and the garden becomes an extension of the home's interior.

Photography by Ethan Kaplan and Joe Fletcher

Alex and Ivan Terry - TERRY & TERRY ARCHITECTURE   1073 Euclid Ave Berkeley, CA 94708 USA   Phone: +1 510 525 0504

www.terryandterryarchitecture.com

CAMELIA COTTAGE

KEVIN HUI
Designer

21 Villiers Street
North Melbourne VIC 3051 AUS

Phone: +61 3 9329 6011

www.4site-architecture.com

ABOUT THE DESIGNER

Kevin Hui is the Melbourne director of 4site Architecture. He also founded the online architecture forum pushpullbar.com in 2004, which focuses on design through critique.

He is a keen architectural traveler, often embarking on 'archi-marathons' around the world and using the exposure to and experiences of architecture as a springboard for his designs and for his teachings at various universities.

4site Architecture has an interest in clever and compact architecture, with sensitivity to site and cultural contexts.

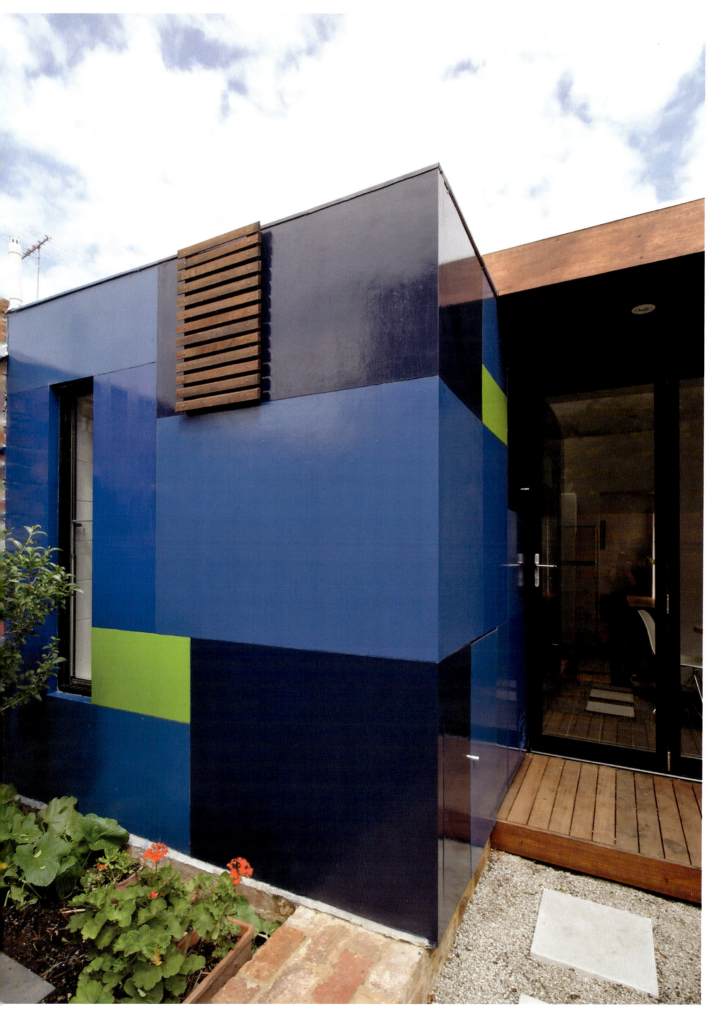

The Project: Reworking inner city terrace houses is always a challenge and this project at 4site Melbourne was no exception. The house was small, as was the site, which made the organization of space crucial to the eventual environment of the home.

While respecting the quality of the space within the existing terrace house, designer Kevin Hui was adamant the new insertion at the rear of the property be dramatic and obvious. A rare blossom in a monotonous heritage area.

It is the graphic and colourful joinery unit that defines the rear extension's distinctive personality, visually connecting the inside to the outside in a way that make the two seem one.

When the adjoining bi-folding doors are open, the afore mentioned visual connection becomes a physical one, opening up the two reasonably restricted spaces to make a larger whole, articulated and made finer by the break-up of colours to the joinery unit.

Each new element in the home is geared toward this illusion of space. A glass splashback was added to the simple laminex kitchen, bringing a sense of depth to the narrow space through reflections. Similarly, window placement has been considered in such a way that it brings as much natural light into the home's core as possible.

A lean-to on one side of the living room creates an informal sunroom. Light pours in from above, bouncing of the white walls and pale timber floor that flows down into the living area, enclosing storage below and providing additional seating. In this living room, the chimney was removed, though the memory of the old fireplace remains in the design of the storage wall. The original bricks were left in the same location as where the hearth once was and now houses the entertainment suite.

Even though the house was small to start with, the additional spaces similarly needed to be tight, as there was little or no room to expand to. Through clever, simple and logical space planning however, the once convoluted spaces have become effortless with movement now easy through a house that seems a lot more spacious.

Photography by Kevin Hui

GARDINER HOUSE

ABOUT THE PROJECT

The existing property was typical of an early 20th century worker's cottage, with a poorly planned series of gloomy, dysfunctional lean-to additions, no access to natural light and no direct connection to the rear yard. Though there were two useable bedrooms and a small living area, the clients requested a new bathroom, laundry, kitchen and dining area that was more livable and that made the most of the site's limited solar access and opened to a private outdoor space.

Responding to the site's limited conditions, Kevin Hui of 4site Melbourne designed a services core that contained the bathroom and laundry. This allowed the higher volume area that is the kitchen and dining room to be positioned at the rear of the house for direct connection to the yard.

Formally, the addition consists of two elements connected by a small hallway. The first is a white box, containing the new bathroom and laundry, the second a black metal-clad box houses an open-plan kitchen and dining area. The latter reaches up over the former by way of a skillion roof that terminates in a clerestory window to the north. This maximises the amount of sunlight, both direct and bounced off the sloping ceiling, giving the new addition a warmth and openness that overcome the constraints of the site.

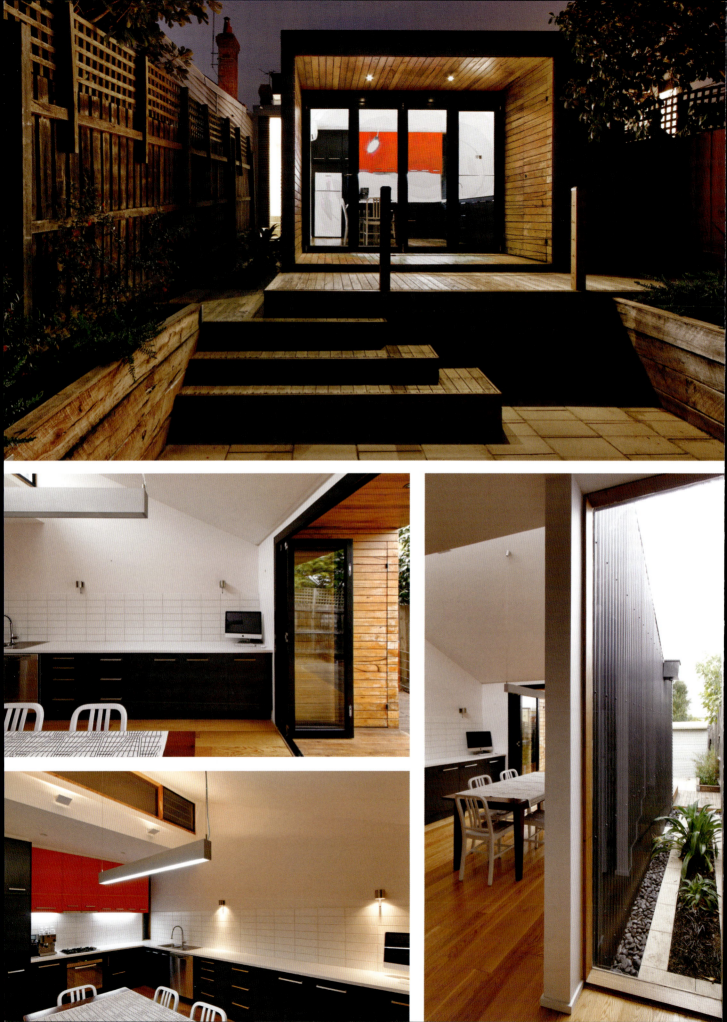

The Project: Connection from the kitchen and dining area to the outside is amplified by the framing of the rear yard by a low, beautifully proportioned timber-clad verandah that temporarily compresses one's view and passage before releasing it to the small backyard beyond. Past this, a series of timber decks lead down to a paved area perfect for summer entertaining.

Upon entry to the house, one is presented with a view to the rear courtyard through a full height window at the termination of the hallway. This gives an immediate sense of light and flow through the house. The inclusion of a side timber slot panel also allows for cross-ventilation whilst providing insect screening and security, a simple and economical device that was inspired by the simplicity of 1950's Modernism.

Transition between the existing cottage and the new addition is marked via the compression and release of ceiling heights. High ceilings become much lower in the hallway, and then open up again upon entry to the kitchen and dining area. The visual shift amplifies the sense of height and openness and strengthens the delineation between the new and the old.

Photography by Kevin Hui

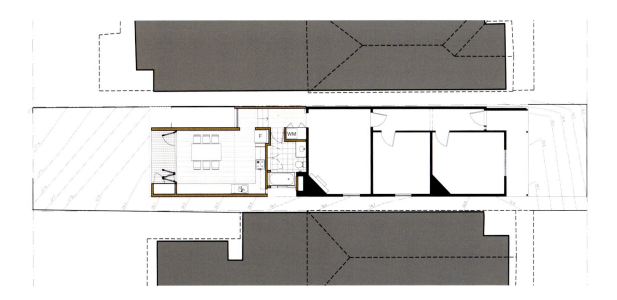

BY THE BAY

BENNI TRAJCEVSKI
Designer

451 Melbourne Road
Newport VIC 3015 AUS

Phone: +61 3 9391 0166

www.achievedesign.com.au

ABOUT THE DESIGNER

Benni Trajcevski formed Achieve Design Group in 1996. Since this time he has established himself as one of the leading designers in Melbourne's West, specialising in custom designed homes, multi-unit developments and apartment buildings. Always demonstrating design versatility and flair in a professional manner, the practice has been rewarded with multiple industry awards, demonstrating Benni's strong work ethic and performance.

As he strives to be sensitive to the individual requirements of each project, his innovative and exciting approach to contemporary and period architecture has earned him the respect and praise of both his peers and clients alike.

His proudest achievement, however, is managing his busy office while at the same time being a great father to his two daughters. Being a parent and understanding what a family home requires has helped to enhance his effectiveness in developing practical and functional building designs. By working efficiently through impressive time and team management protocols, Benni has given his clients the most functional designs possible at an affordable budget.

The Project: On a small lot of just 188 square metres, Achieve Design Group has established this contemporary Williamstown home that lacks nothing in the way of function and design. The harmonious forms and consideration of all elements are important components of the overall design, well articulated through the use of different materials such as steel and render, with the main focus being on the use of glass. The site's modest size has had no effect on the home's ability to create a big impact in the established inner urban area. Housing a growing family, the designer utilised every millimetre possible in the generation of an open plan home with large internal and external spaces for living and entertaining.

The interior uses curves, a mix of natural and new material as well as natural light in forming an impressive three-level house with internal and external living and entertaining zones that flow seamlessly from one to the other. Principle living areas are located on the first floor so that the outlook to the view could be maximised. Municipal guidelines determined the tri-column façade to reflect the heritage overlay and the building envelope restricted the height of the building.

As per the client's brief, the kitchen forms the hub of the living areas. The sharp lines of its striking geometric island bench juxtapose the smoothly curved lower ceiling above. A red glass splashback ties together with other bold red elements through the home. The structure's abstract façade of opaque glass conceals a red tile pond that defines the entrance beneath a soaring void. Other interesting features of the home include the sculptural kitchen and a living area that opens out to a deck housing a sculpture, water feature and red feature wall.

Perhaps the most striking feature of the house is the use of glass. Its placement on the façade ensures the streaming of natural light into the interior spaces. A mixture of translucent, opaque and clear glasses create a façade that has depth and gives privacy and light to the adjacent rooms. Here is a modern town house that will capture the imaginations of generations to come.

Photography by Xenia Michos

Benni Trajcevski - ACHIEVE DESIGN GROUP 451 Melbourne Road Newport VIC 3015 AUS   Phone: +61 3 9391 0166

www.achievedesign.com.au

WARM AND COSY

MARIA GIGNEY
Architect

14 Molle Street,
Hobart TAS 7000 AUS

Phone: +61 3 6223 3446

www.mariagigneyarchitects.com

ABOUT THE ARCHITECT

Maria graduated from UTAS in 1992 with a Bachelor of Environmental Design and a Bachelor of Architecture (Honours). Following university, Maria worked with Philip Lighton in Launceston for two years, followed by five years at Heffernan Button Vos. In 1999 she founded her own company, Maria Gigney Architects, and became the youngest female sole practitioner in Hobart, Australia.

Architecture proved to be the right choice for Maria, who has been widely recognised as a leader in her field. "We have been winning Tasmanian Architecture Awards in residential categories since 2000. The greatest achievement in this area was when we won the National Architecture Awards Category for Small Project Architecture in 2010," she says.

Maria recognises that architecture is a very labour intensive profession that demands a broad range of skills. Her success relies on her ability to form strong working relationships, which enable her projects to run smoothly.

The Project: Tucked behind a Federation house, this once dilapidated little barn is now a cosy apartment. Restored without changing much of the building fabric itself, the barn is a stylish small residence with a sensitive interior treatment that brings out the character in the existing features.

Although not heritage listed in its own right, the barn presumably dates back to the 1840s. It was thus highly desirable to maintain the integrity of the structure and utilize or

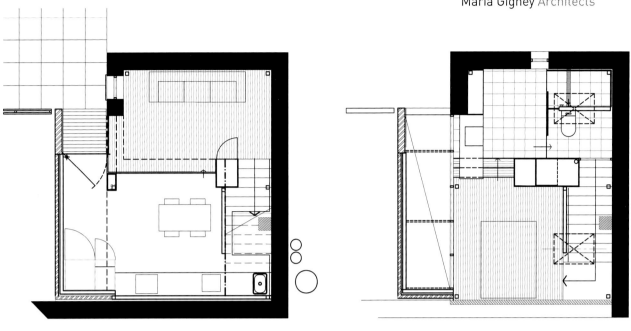

GROUND FLOOR   FIRST FLOOR

reuse as many of the original elements as possible. Given the dreadful state of the structure, this was an enormous challenge. With no real need to extend, the barn's original built form remains dominant with only minor additions. A new timber-clad entry wall and an adjacent glass roof form a welcoming entrance to the building.

Inside, a new roof was built above the existing one on an independent steel portal frame, enabling the retention of the original roof framing now visible inside the barn.

Creaky and unstable, the original mezzanine was removed. The timber flooring was inverted and reused as the ceiling lining for the living area, simply cleaned and oiled to maintain its visual integrity. Once climbing to the mezzanine level, a ladder has been reused as a towel rack in the bathroom. The original floor joists were made into a table for the dining area.

The barn's inherent quirks were treated as advantages to the rather special new design. The walls and roof were not straightened, holes where original elements had been were left and the rising damp was treated and concealed behind joinery. Extensive use of timber to the interior is the perfect complement to the exposed stone walls, together creating a warm and cosy palette of interior materials complemented only by a few select new elements that have turned the building into a home.

Photography by Matthew Newton

Maria Gigney - MARIA GIGNEY ARCHITECTS   14 Molle Street, Hobart TAS 7000 AUS   Phone: +61 3 6223 3446

www.mariagigneyarchitects.com

ST KILDA WEST

ROYSTON WILSON
Designer

Suite 4/927 High Street,
Armadale VIC 3143

Phone: +61 3 9822 3173

roystonwilson.com.au

ABOUT THE DESIGNER

Royston Wilson has had a checkered career spanning more that two decades.
Famous for his unique bathroom and kitchen designs, he also uses his creative prowess
in the area of building design to create complete homes and bespoke extensions.

Wilson, considered a leader not a follower, attributes his success to an amalgamation of
factors: surrounding himself with like-minded designers, regularly attending overseas
fairs and exhibitions, drawing inspiration from the history of design, always re-inventing
and improving, and most importantly, listening to his clients requests, understanding
their needs and then committing to delivering their dream.

As an internationally recognised designer, Wilson has enjoyed commissions
outside of Australia. "Working in countries such as the United Kingdom, the
Middle East and America certainly has its challenges, but the projects were
exciting at the same time," he says.

When asked what his philosophy is, Wilson has said, "That's easy – integrity in business,
inspiration in design and unparalleled commitment to my clients."

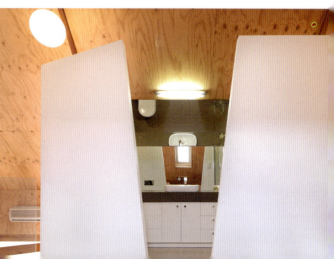

The Project: This small bedroom addition within the confines of an established home is chic and sophisticated, with that edgy sensibility one comes to expect from homes in the trendy suburb of St Kilda, Melbourne.

Within this stylish residence, Royston Wilson was given the job to add an additional bedroom, en suite and walk-in robe. This seemed reasonably straight forward, but there was a catch - the addition could not be outside the existing building envelope. Responding to the challenge, Wilson conceived a plan that saw the bedroom fitted into the lofty ceiling space, which tops the living area and carries on over the kitchen and dining room zones.

The resulting design is unique in many ways, in that it appears to simply float within the ceiling space, creating a remarkably open and spacious atmosphere despite the existing space constraints and the need to retain the plywood ceiling.

Carriage up to this level is via a timber stairway, which is set against painted exposed brick and guarded by a seamless glass balustrade. This balustrade ensures the bedroom, though private, remains open to the remainder of the roof space and takes in the outlook to the rear below.

Angular and freestanding white walls stop short of the steeply raking ceiling, practically but effectively concealing the en suite and walk-in robe. The placement of these walls and their individual designs achieves the functional outcomes of the secondary rooms without encroaching on the visual sense of space.

Clever detailing of the small en suite – particularly with the use of mirrors – maximises space and avoids awkward wall to ceiling junctions.

This project is a highly creative response to the constraints of working within a small, existing space. Designer Royston Wilson has treated those constraints as opportunities and with a few simple but deft strokes has created a functional and beautiful living space.

Photography by Andrew Ashton

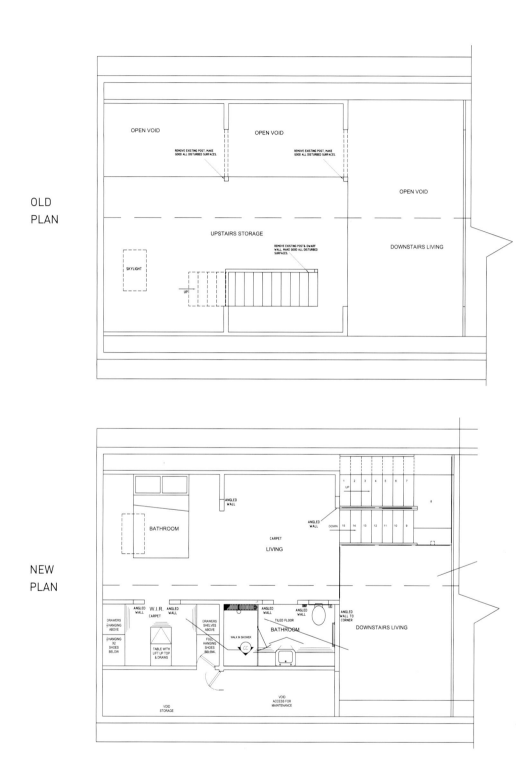

OLD
PLAN

OPEN VOID

OPEN VOID

REMOVE EXISTING POST. MAKE
GOOD ALL DISTURBED SURFACES.

REMOVE EXISTING POST. MAKE
GOOD ALL DISTURBED SURFACES.

OPEN VOID

UPSTAIRS STORAGE

DOWNSTAIRS LIVING

REMOVE EXISTING POST & DWARF
WALL, MAKE GOOD ALL DISTURBED
SURFACES.

SKYLIGHT

UP

NEW
PLAN

ANGLED
WALL

BATHROOM

ANGLED
WALL

CARPET

LIVING

UP

DOWN

ANGLED
WALL

DRAWERS
HANGING
ABOVE

ANGLED
WALL

W.I.R.
CARPET

ANGLED
WALL

DRAWERS
SHELVES
ABOVE

ANGLED
WALL

TILED FLOOR

ANGLED
WALL

ANGLED
WALL TO
CORNER

DOWNSTAIRS LIVING

HANGING
X2
SHOES
BELOW

TABLE WITH
LIFT UP TOP
& DRAWS

FULL
HANGING
SHOES
BELOW

WALK IN SHOWER

BATHROOM

VOID
STORAGE

VOID
ACCESS FOR
MAINTENANCE

FITZROY STREET

PAUL DI STEFANO
Designer

53 Ormond Road,
East Geelong VIC 3220 AUS

Phone: +61 3 5221 3302

pauldistefanodesign.com

Following a decade of experience in a small architectural office, Paul Di Stefano Design was established in 2006. Specialising in residential space, Paul's unique approach to domestic architecture begins with care and commitment to nurturing the relationships with his clients through the exciting journey of creating a unique and special residential environment.

He approaches projects individually, personally and with due respect to project brief and budget. Drawing from various influences – particularly contemporary Japanese and modern Pacific architecture as well as the natural qualities of materials – Paul's residential work demonstrates a vision from conception that clarifies and articulates a residence's unique relationship to its local context. He regards the design process as a careful balancing and fine-tuning of aesthetics, practicalities, priorities and compromises. The challenge of achieving delight within constraint is relished as is converting constraint into design opportunity.

Projects are understood as complex collaborations of numerous people, specialists and trades where communication between all involved is paramount to the process and its success. Attention to detail throughout all stages of the construction process ensures consistency of style from the large to small-scale elements and consequently ensures that the architecture created by Paul will be rewarding on all levels.

The Project: A family owned site that remained vacant for over 40 years, became the perfect canvas for Paul Di Stefano's unique design - a light-filled, spatially articulated but compact house that is now home to his young family.

The contemporary building form draws direct influence from the traditional dwelling style and scale of the neighbourhood's dwellings. The realised aesthetic however is clean and streamlined, housing two storeys within a single storey profile. This was achieved by setting the ground floor slightly lower than natural ground level and incorporating a bedroom in an attic type space created below the gable roof.

A timber boardwalk through the landscaped garden bypasses the house's private areas, leading guests directly into the main living area at the rear. The engaging vista through to the rear courtyard gives the experience of space and light in what would otherwise be seen as a tight space. Interesting light quality and framed outlooks articulate the internal spaces via carefully considered apertures throughout the residence, of particular note abundant fenestration around the Living area, and creative roof glazing to the main bathroom, laundry and upper bedroom.

Spatial proportions are over emphasized in the main living zone. What Paul has achieved here is the feeling of space beyond expectation, with an emphasised ceiling height articulated by internally expressed roof pitches. The main living area features glazed cedar-framed doors that, when open, seamlessly integrate and connect the outdoor living area. Floor to ceiling glazing brings natural light into the living area, as do a series of high-level windows. A narrow, low maintenance feature garden slotted to the northern side of the living room is framed within a large window next to the dining table, becoming a three dimensional picture of greenery particularly enjoyed at night with external feature garden lighting.

Striking and dramatic, the exposed gable roof extends over the living zone into the attic-style bedroom above. Cosy and intimate, the bedroom makes for an interesting use of space within the home's tight profile.

An abundance of practical storage at every possible opportunity allows the series of spaces to feel uncluttered and open, despite their relatively small scale. A practical home office nook is achieved within a small, widened passage under the stairs.

The success of the house is not a result of specifying expensive fittings or materials. Rather, it is the articulation and balance of every space through carefully considered detailing, and making the most of every opportunity to express the spaces in an interesting and fresh manner.

Photography by The Geelong Advertiser, Naomi Di Stefano, Paul Di Stefano

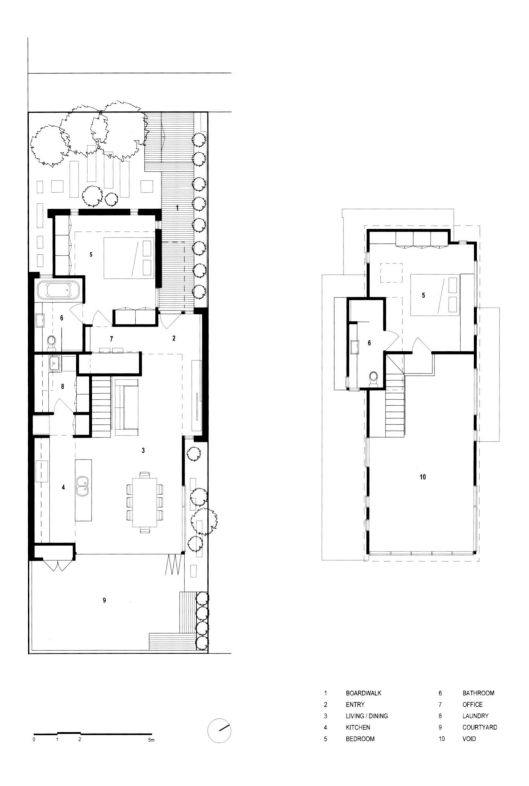

1	BOARDWALK	6	BATHROOM
2	ENTRY	7	OFFICE
3	LIVING / DINING	8	LAUNDRY
4	KITCHEN	9	COURTYARD
5	BEDROOM	10	VOID

RIPPLESIDE RESIDENCE

MARK SANDERS
Architect

The Beehive, 1/216
Pakington Street Geelong
West VIC 3218 AUS

Phone: +61 3 5229 8361

www.thirdecology.com.au

Mark Sanders, Managing Director of Third Ecology, has a simple philosophy – work closely with clients to create highly sustainable projects that minimize their impact on nature. His goal is to mainstream the use and adoption of ESD (Environmentally Sustainable Design) principles.

Through Third Ecology, Mark has built a team of professionals who are highly capable, dedicated and passionate about this cause and prove time and time again that ecological sustainable design can be aesthetically stimulating and functional while respecting the land and most importantly transforming the lives of those who dwell in it.

Third Ecology is an award winning, multi-disciplinary team who specialize in architecture and master planning, construction and sustainability advice and rating services. The diverse group provides clients with one of the most complete and extensive ranges of service when it comes to creating their sought-after projects.

The Project: After following the work of Third Ecology for many years, the owners of this small site on Victoria's Ballerine Peninsula approached the firm to design and build a modest, highly sustainable and above all livable home.

The 203m2 Rippleside Residence is nestled between homes of varying eras, so it was important for it to set itself apart in both form and materials. To this end, a contemporary but simple form was developed with the expression of natural features both inside and out creating an unexpected 1950's retro feel. Silvertop Ash shiplap cladding provides warmth to the streetscape as well as announcing the home's intent to subtly stand out from its neighbours.

Sitting comfortably and unobtrusively on its site, the home is nestled into the landform, creating an instant, protected outdoor environment around the perimeter. This allows for easy access to the exterior from the ground floor both at the front and rear.

The house makes ideal use of its north facing rear garden with living areas spilling onto the north facing deck. Glimpses of views to the coast are provided from the secondary living space at the front of the property.

Sustainability was high on the agenda when it came to selecting materials. Paints and other applied finishes are low VOC, timbers are recycled or from sustainable origins, concrete features a high level of recycled aggregate and high performance double glazing and high levels of wall and ceiling insulation were used throughout. Similarly all fixtures and fittings were chosen with energy and water efficiency in mind. A solar panel PV system generates the home's electricity.

On the ground level is an open-plan kitchen, living and dining space, a separate sitting room that could be converted to a bedroom should future need arise, a home office, a bathroom and a laundry integrated into the pantry for effective use of limited space. Polished, exposed aggregate concrete flooring to this level pairs beautifully with the recycled Australian hardwoods used extensively for bench tops and joinery.

Two bedrooms, en suite and separate bathroom form the upper level. Timber stairs ascend from below to a landing and walkway of polished, recycled hardwood that allows light to filter through the floor to the entry below. A large void above the ground floor living area gives it spatial volume with highlight windows letting natural light deep into the internal spaces.

Simple in form and slight in size, the Rippleside Residence by Third Ecology lacks nothing in the way of design – proving that sustainability, livability and visual appeal can work in harmony.

Photographer: Open2View Photography

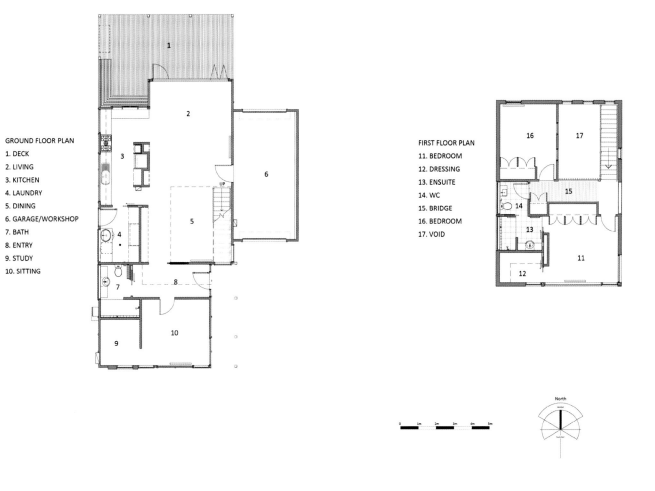

GROUND FLOOR PLAN
1. DECK
2. LIVING
3. KITCHEN
4. LAUNDRY
5. DINING
6. GARAGE/WORKSHOP
7. BATH
8. ENTRY
9. STUDY
10. SITTING

FIRST FLOOR PLAN
11. BEDROOM
12. DRESSING
13. ENSUITE
14. WC
15. BRIDGE
16. BEDROOM
17. VOID

North

0   1m   2m   3m   4m   5m

THE BLUE HOUSE

NATHALIE SCIPIONI
Designer

11A Fredbert Street,
Lilyfield NSW 2040 AUS

Phone: +61 2 9818 2237

www.ns-studio.com

ABOUT THE DESIGNER

Nathalie Scipioni received her PHD in Architecture from the University of Florence, Italy, with a thesis on the history of the castle of Caen. She worked 10 years in Paris, where she received a post graduate diploma in heritage architecture at the 'Ecole de Chaillot'. She relocated to Sydney seven years ago, working in heritage, residential and commercial architecture, and started her own practice in 2008 as a building designer, interior designer and heritage consultant. Nathalie applies her skills in every field of architecture and interior design, including residential renovations, new houses, hospitality and commercial projects.

When she works on a renovation project, Nathalie believes that the original features must be conserved alongside the new additions, so as to contrast the differences between the past and the present. "Old and modern can work very well together," she says. Nathalie is always on the lookout for new materials, and likes to put some Italian and French design aesthetics in her projects.

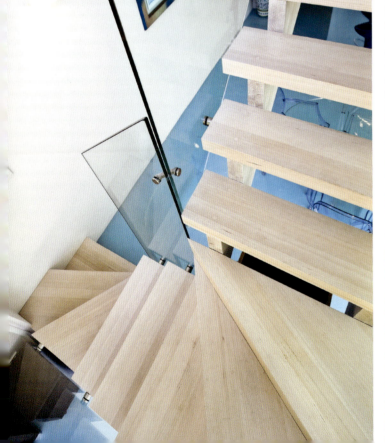

The Project: This 1920s brick cottage was in very poor condition, with replacement or restoration required for close to every aspect. Now aptly named 'The Blue House,' the cottage is alight with luminosity, colour and above all, character.

Much of the rear of the original cottage was demolished to make way for a graceful new addition encompassing kitchen, dining and living area, plus a stair up to a new first floor. The first floor houses a master bedroom with en suite, walk-in-robe, studio and terrace overlooking the rear garden.

After moving past the revamped façade, the innate monotony of the long corridor is broken up by a most surprising turquoise floor and accented recessed wall lighting. This sea of colour underfoot spreads out through the living spaces, taking on the premier role in the area as it contrasts with the whiteness of everything else. Recessed alcoves that house the entertainment suite and knick knacks are backed by a dark sparkling blue that similarly creates a strong contrast.

Ascending its timber treads up to the first floor, the stair in itself is a primary feature of the space. By wrapping it in glass walls, light can filter through ensuring the structure remains ever so light.

Folding glass doors and expanses of windows brighten the living zone, as do the playful furniture choices. Lighting and colour have played a very important role in this project and its interior.

The three bathrooms have each been treated in a different way. One en suite to a children's room has flower motifs, while the redone original bathroom features a white smooth wash plane underlined by a mirror and silver tiles that reflect light. The en suite to the master bedroom features the same sparkling colour of the adjacent bedroom feature wall.

Different light fittings in each room reflect the colour and typology of the spaces they inhabit. Pendant lights are predominant in the high ceiling of the original house.

The entire idea of the project was to maintain and restore the beautiful original features of an old house using modern materials, creating a completely modern and contemporary space with an accented contrast between old and new.

Photography by Kevin Chamberlain Photography and Tim Whiteman

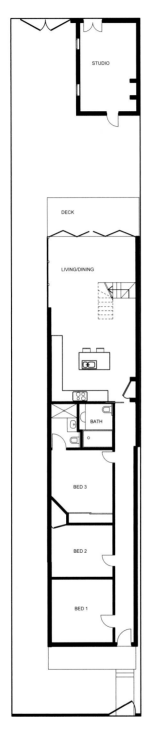

Ground Floor

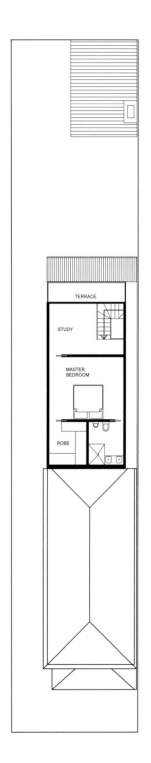

First Floor

Nathalie Scipioni - NSSTUDIO   1A Fredbert Street Lilyfield NSW 2040 AUS   Phone: +61 2 9818 2237

www.ns-studio.com

ART HOUSE ONE

KYLIE MITCHELL
Designer

68 Butler Street Armidale
NSW 2350 AUS
Phone: +61 407 126 659

www.kyliemitchell.com.au

ABOUT THE DESIGNER

Kylie Mitchell is a qualified Building, Interiors and Permaculture Designer who offers her clients the complete package for their homes.

Working on renovations, extensions and new houses equally, her passion for residential housing sparked a particular interest in compact, sustainable design with visual art influences – being an exhibiting artist herself, this is something she understands intimately. Kylie believes in creating spaces that work and that are easy and enjoyable to live in, all the while challenging people to think outside the box with regards to their personal impact on the environment.

Having raised a family, Kylie understands the way houses have to work on a practical, day-to-day level and believes very strongly in spaces that can adapt to a variety of uses to suit the ever-changing needs of their inhabitants. As such, she places a strong emphasis on practicality and streamlining household functions. This includes designing to streamline the building and approval processes as much as possible, so that creating one's dream home is as stress free as possible.

The Project: Designed as a live-in artwork, Art House One is a modern house designed around a single abstract art theme developed by the designer Kylie Mitchell. Its purpose was to create a compact, environmentally sensitive building that was easy to use, cheap to build and that would act as a canvas to carry the art theme into every aspect of the occupant's life.

What Art House One has done is change the concept of art from an object and its related experience to a daily, living environment and a day-to-day intimate experience.

The modest 527/sq block lead to a 'micro-design', incorporating a strong street presence and a comfortably sized and sited house, the individual design quality of which Kylie hopes will encourage people to really think about how much space is actually required for comfortable, healthy lifestyle.

Building costs were dramatically reduced by the small plan and simple construction techniques, which in turn reduced building time and waste, environmental impact, heating and cooling costs as well as consumerism since there is far less space to fill with 'stuff'.

Though the home stands out as something unique, everyday materials were used to create the artwork to the façade. The simple shape of the building itself was also vital as it formed a canvas for the artwork.

Inside, all wasted space is eradicated, while freedom of movement and storage is more than catered for. The art theme flows from room to room, each space reflecting a different interpretation while maintaining the simple colour format - red. This includes abstract wall murals, feature tiling, bright red doors, windows and carpet as well as furniture and decoration items. The subtlety and simplicity of the compact design makes for the perfect backdrop to highlight the artwork while also grounding it with practical application to everyday life.

All products used have a modern, simple appearance with a focus on combining texture, surface and colour. Materials were chosen for their suitability to the art theme, but also based on the environmental sensitivity of the object and the company by which the object was produced.

Northern orientation sees sunlight pour into the house, warming the polished concrete floor, which acts as a thermal mass. Double glazed windows, crafted by a local company, provide insulation. All the paints used are low VOC. Water that runs off the roof areas is collected for use in the garden and laundry. 4 Star tap fittings and instantaneous gas hot water reduce water usage within the home. New appliances have been selected for their energy efficiency.

The house is a show piece to encourage people to think of their properties from a different angle – to promote conversation and action around reducing the environmental impact of buildings while creating unique individual homes, all within a sensible budget.

Photography by Simon Scott Photography

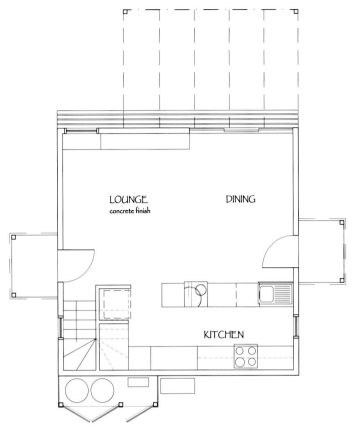

Ground Floor

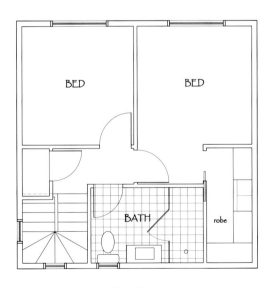

Top Floor

SOUTH MELBOURNE HOUSE

ROB WATSON
Architect

3 / 376 Albert Street
East Melbourne VIC 3002, AUS

Phone: +61 3 9417 7275

www.watsonarchitecture.com

ABOUT THE ARCHITECT

Australian born Rob Watson has degrees in both Industrial Design and Architecture, establishing his multi-discipline practice in Melbourne in 1997.

Prior to that, he spent a number of years working in London for two renowned practices on high profile projects such as the British Pavilion for the 1992 world Expo in Seville, Spain when working for Grimshaw, and the Reichstag re-development for Germany's new parliament after unification in Berlin when working for Foster and Partners.

Rob Watson's practice works on a wide range projects from private houses, infrastructure and product design, through to providing pro bono architectural services to an Australian NGO building children's homes in East Africa.

Rob Watson believes that design is a field of endeavour that explores the meaning of elegance – a response to a problem and the clarity in which the response is achieved.

Neither style nor theme enters Watson's work, he leaves that for others to determine. Hence in this project, the house is purposely understated and restrained. Slotted neatly amidst Victorian terrace houses, this two-bedroom dwelling boasts simple, calm lines that see its modern nature blend seamlessly with the heritage streetscape.

White aluminium composite cladding panels and natural anodized commercial section window frames set between natural cement rendered full height walls comprise the front elevation that spans just 4.8 metres. At the other end of the 21.7 metres long property, the rear elevation uses the same materials, set off by a bespoke screen made up of translucent glass louvers.

Internally, the palette of materials is restrained. Throughout the ground floor is a polished concrete slab that forms that base for a contemporary ensemble of materials including timber and glass. Extensive built-in joinery completes the simple, uniformed interior landscape.

A unique element the house is a 5.3 metre long clear glass floor on the first level that lets natural light down to the ground floor from a matching translucent-glazed skylight above – combating the challenge of the narrow, long plan's east-west orientation and transforming the spaces inside.

The interior design revolves around a central compact core existing of the fully enclosed flight of stairs, corridors and service areas clad in American Oak veneer panels with a natural wax finish. These elements were kept as compact as possible to afford the other rooms more space. Living and dining rooms comprise the ground floor and two bedrooms the first. A small study makes a third level linked to a rooftop deck, and a rear courtyard extends out from the living area.

Every inch of space has been carefully considered, planned and utilized in this slight home that encompasses everything necessary for modern living and more.

Photography by Patrick Redmond

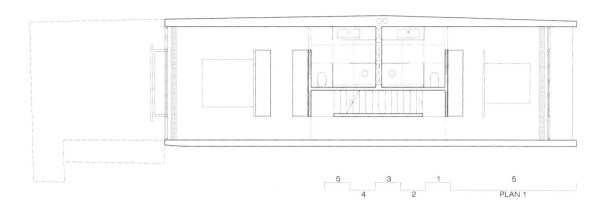

5   3   1   5
  4   2   PLAN 1

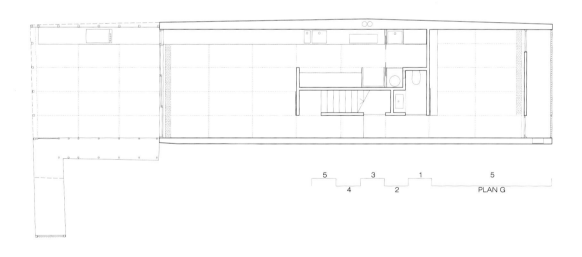

5   3   1   5
  4   2   PLAN G

Rob Watson - WATSONARCHITECTURE+DESIGN   3 / 376 Albert Street, East Melbourne VIC 3002, AUS

Phone: +61 3 9417 7275   www.watsonarchitecture.com

WARRNAMBOOL WOOLEN MILL REDEVELOPMENT

CHRIS STEEL
Designer

202 Lava St
Warrnambool VIC 3280 AUS

Phone: +61 3 5561 3444

www.steelandtippett.com.au

ABOUT THE DESIGNER

Building Designer Chris Steel – managing director of Steel and Tippett Building Designers – has had over 24 years of design experience since he began as a junior draughtsman for a local building firm in 1987. Chris began his own building design firm in 1991 before forming a partnership with former colleague Paul Tippett in 1996.

Steel and Tippett is an innovative design firm providing building solutions to South West Victoria in Australia. They have been developing a widely recognized design portfolio for over 15 years, and specialize in residential, commercial, renovation and industrial projects.

With excellence in producing comfortable, stylish and environmentally sensitive designs, Steel and Tippett Building Designers consider clients' briefs, lifestyle and environmental factors integral to producing exceptional buildings.

The Project: Designed as part of a redevelopment project at the old woolen mill site in Warrnambool in Victoria, this dwelling was to be a single story residence appealing to retirees or singles, comprising two bedrooms or a single bedroom and a study. Steel and Tippett Building Designers have created a small, modern home that feels spacious and light-filled and satisfies all the modern desires for seamless living.

Part of a development of seven similar houses, the design would set the standard for the new, establishing streetscape. Hence careful consideration was given to achieve a fresh and contemporary look not only in the house's architecture but also to the smart front fence and landscaping.

The compact but versatile design of the residences allows for plenty of room to move, with sloping ceiling and highlight windows achieving a sense of space in the tight area. Glazing is implemented to full advantage with its sensible and economical use capturing northern sunlight and adding façade appeal, particularly when incorporated into the large box window articulated in eye-catching lime green.

Front and rear private courtyards provide the kind of outdoor living experience necessary to the modern Australian lifestyle. A slightly cantilevered roof provides shade and protection to the bluestone lain front courtyard and entry, made private behind the timber and render fence. A second, private outdoor space is incorporated to the rear of the house of the living zone.

Atop Bamboo timber flooring, the open plan living and dining areas abut the surprisingly spacious kitchen, next to which a space-saving European laundry is hidden from sight. The living and dining areas are not only flooded with light but also enjoy a view and access to the rear outdoor space, a feature that permits effortless entertaining.

Photography by Dean Kilpatrick of Oyster Images

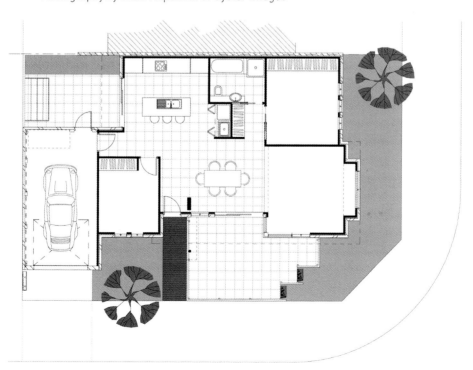

DRIFTWOOD BEACH HOUSE

PAUL HINDES
Designer

23 Paluma Street
Sunrise Beach QLD 4567 AUS

Phone: +61 7 5455 3651

www.soulspace.com.au

ABOUT THE DESIGNER

Soul Space Building Design is a vibrant and enthusiastic architectural practice with a strong commitment to providing excellent quality architectural design and comprehensive documentation services. The practice specialises in residential and commercial buildings as well as office and shop fitouts. Soul Space works closely with a diverse range of clients in providing creative, innovative and contemporary architectural design.

Principle Designer Paul Hindes has some 30 years experience in the profession, gaini valuable experience working with award winning Architects John Andrews Internation Edwards Madigan Torzillo Briggs, DEM and Inscan Design, as well as overseas experience in El Salvador.

In 1988 Paul established his documentation business and rapidly built up a reputation for quality architectural documentation. He formed Soul Space in 2004, designing quality homes. Operating from his Noosa based studio on the Sunshine Coast in Queensland, Australia, Paul works in close partnership with his clients to achieve their dream home within budget.

The Project: A contemporary take on the quintessential Australian beach shack, this visually large but physically petite house captures the holiday atmosphere the owners so desired. Expressed through a variety of contemporary, lightweight materials, the engaging façade offers but a mere taste of the highly designed, modern interior that unfolds upon entry.

The façade's stand out element – the high, pitched roof to the centre – shelters a double height entryway from where the home's two stories ascend and descend, a layout conceived to combat the front to back 2m gradient of the land. Division of the two stories both makes flow between the two easy and creates a link that makes the home seem larger than it really is.

Here, the palette of natural interiors used throughout is immediately realised with granite tiles contrasted with pale timber stairs. Following the downward steps, one is brought to a spilt level living space comprising lounge, dining and kitchen, whose bright white fabric is the perfect expression of the seaside atmosphere.

Beyond the lounge area, the home opens to an outdoor alfresco area adjacent to the pool – the perfect spot for a mid-summer afternoon barbeque and swim. Nestled tightly between the fence and garage, the simple swimming pool becomes a feature of the outdoor area, with ambiant sounds radiating from the stylish waterfall into the pool. Visibility of the water is seamless with glass balustrading.

The adjacent paved alfresco area is punctuated by squares of the grass that replace the odd paver. This feature is a great way to bring living elements into a design that had to be low maintenance.

Overhead, a bedroom and study extend beyond the ground floor footprint to provide cover to the outdoor entertaining area below. Upstairs, careful planning of the bedrooms and study allow for an open gallery at the top of the stairs.

Photography provided by Soul Space

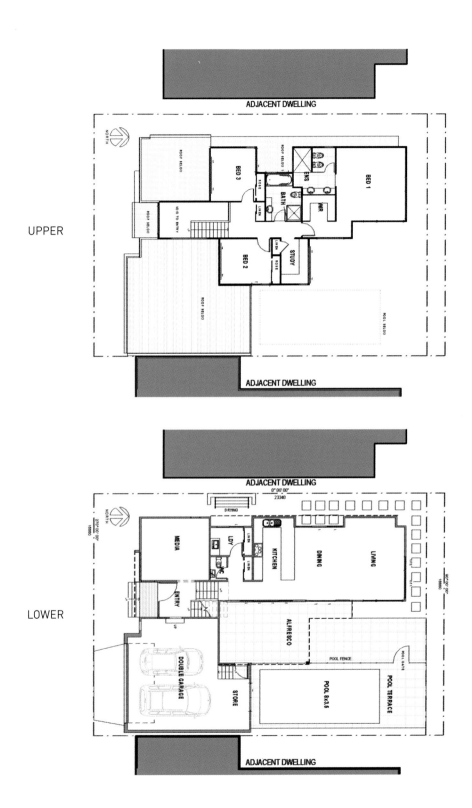

UPPER

LOWER

Paul Hindes- SOUL SPACE   23 Paluma Street Sunrise Beach QLD 4567 AUS   +61 7 5455 3651

FERGUSON STREET

The Project: What was once a tired 80's duplex has been updated by Soul Space into an open, flowing beach house that effortlessly integrates outdoor and indoor living with beautifully landscaped courtyards.

The existing building had the living areas upstairs with a large balcony space facing the street, and the bedroom spaces on the lower floor with a dark corridor connecting the bedroom. The apartments were identical, but mirrored.

The design was challenging – the nature of the duplex meant that there were two clients who had two different budgets. Unit one allowed for a complete redesign, putting the living spaces on the lower floor, and two bedrooms and a study space on the top floor, with a large garage out the front. They wanted to have their living space open to a rear garden with a new plunge pool, seamlessly connecting the indoor and outdoor spaces. The unit two clients were only after a renovation of the existing spaces and a new roof over the front balcony.

The challenge was well met, and each apartment has its own distinct identity whilst still appearing as if it is part of a unified building. The design has opened up the space, allowing abundant natural light to enter both sides of the house. The flowing design also allows for cooling breezes.

Open timber stairs and balustrades afford a sense of space to the otherwise constrained rooms.

Privacy from neighbours and the other residents of the duplex was a consideration, and this is afforded by the reversed living spaces. This is further enhanced by a redevelopment of the internal driveways to allow for visitor parking and landscaped privacy between the apartments. The house is also buffered by trees on either side, ensuring privacy from other neighbours.

The apartments have a distinctive identity within a homogenous beach house style design, ensuring comfort and privacy set in the beautifully landscaped courtyard spaces.

Photographer: Paul Smith Photography
Interior Design: Carole Tretheway Design
Builder: John Jameson

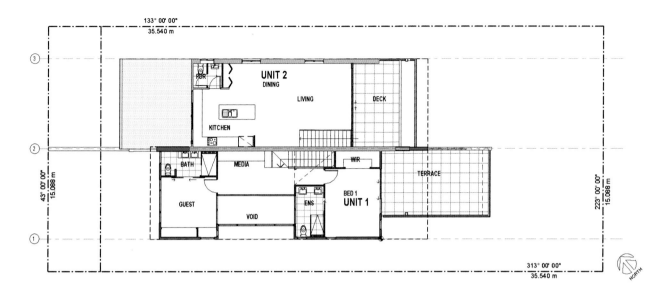

UPPER

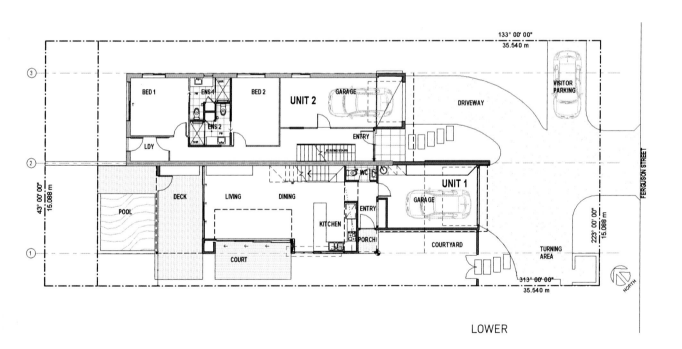

LOWER

Paul Hindes - SOUL SPACE   23 Paluma Street Sunrise Beach QLD 4567 AUS   +61 7 5455 3651

www.soulspace.com.au

TRANSITIONAL RENOVATION

BEN STATKUS
Architect

51 Simpson Street
Northcote VIC 3070 AUS

Phone: +61 3 9482 2201
+61 413 397 715

www.statkusarchitecture.com.au

ABOUT THE ARCHITECT

Ben Statkus is a registered architect who has worked in private practice since 2004. He is the director of Statkus Architecture, a young and energetic architectural practice focused on considered, engaging and sustainably built outcomes. The practice's focus is primarily on quality, client responsive residential projects, involving improvements to existing homes through refurbishments, renovations and extensions for single homes, new homes and multi residential dwellings. The work also extends to government, urban, retail and interior projects.

Since completing his architecture degree at RMIT University with 1st Class Honours, Statkus' work has been featured in numerous publications and exhibitions locally and internationally, including the 2010 Venice Architecture Bienalle, Melbourne Museum and State Ministerial Offices.

Ben has maintained educational links through sessional lecturing and tutoring positions at RMIT University's School of Architecture in design studio, communications and technology.

In recent years, Ben has sought active involvement in community, from efforts in bushfire rebuilding through speculative bushfire rebuilding propositions, voluntary efforts as a Bushfire Attack Level assessor of bushfire affected properties, the design of a community intercultural centre, to participation in teaching kindergarten children eco design through the 2011 Eco Cubby project.

Ben is interested in thoughtful architecture that has the capacity to involve, fulfill and surprise.

This restrained, contemporary re-imagining of a Victorian cottage retains key historical features of the style while introducing a modern extension that aims to complement rather than compete with the existing house, adding as few elements as possible to achieve the final result. Fluid transition between the clean, contemporary interior and the uncluttered exterior intimate a perfectly realised and well organised, stylish design.

This project represents the first and second of three stages, preconceived in a master plan. The first stage involved the implementation of a new kitchen, the second an extension of the study and renovation of the courtyard end of the house.

The functional briefs (stages one and two) were to replace the kitchen, provide adjacent dining area, cosy second living area, study, shed, rainwater harvesting and courtyard landscape works. Stage three works will comprise a reconfiguration of the existing main bedroom to incorporate walk in robe, en suite, and roof storage along with a renovated bathroom and laundry.

The number of different building elements was minimised to decrease the sense of visual clutter, while increasing the sense of space. The façade comprises a frameless operable glass wall with transparent compression seals between the glazed panels.
This beautiful feature has the ability to open up the façade between living and courtyard with minimal tracks.

The courtyard travertine has been laid on a raised concrete slab to match the floor level of the house, increasing the connectivity between the interior and exterior. The travertine paving wraps up the only section of flat 'wall' connecting the two elements, minimising the differentiation between vertical and horizontal surfaces.

The courtyard is deconstructed with a side shed façade and secret door clad in vertical fins to reduce the solidity of the component. A rainwater tank is hidden behind the shed.

The composition of the gas fire and wall recessed television create a clean, and modern feature in the living space that makes an otherwise elegantly simple room a cosy living space for the family. The double-glazed, argon gas filled skylights provide sky access and natural light while reducing heat loss. Remotely operated skylight blockout blinds are to be installed to reduce heat gain in the warmer months.

Conversation between the indoor and outdoor and a fluent use of historical notes to enhance the contemporary façade create a sense of space that the lot didn't afford, resulting in a beautiful, functional and sustainable living space.

Photography by Matthew Mallett

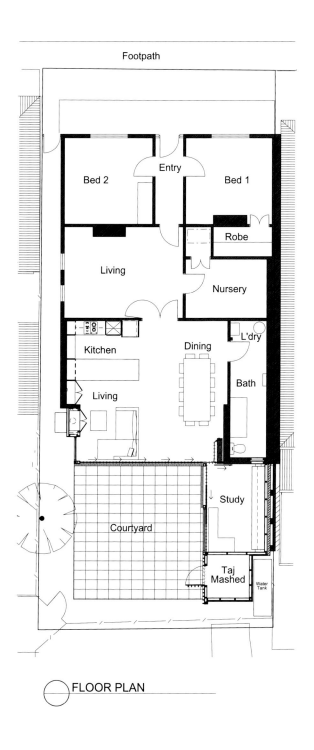

Footpath

Bed 2

Entry

Bed 1

Robe

Living

Nursery

Kitchen

Dining

L'dry

Living

Bath

Courtyard

Study

Taj
Mashed

Water
Tank

◯ FLOOR PLAN

Ben Statkus - Statkus Architecture   51 Simpson Street Northcote VIC 3070 AUS   Phone: +61 3 9482 2201

www.statkusarchitecture.com.au

Front cover photography:

David Mikhail Architects, Photography by Tim Crocker

Back cover photography:

Ian Moore Architects, Photography by Iain D. MacKenzie

All floor plans contained within this book remain
Copyright of their respective owners and designers.

Houses for Small Spaces is published by Think Publishing

ABN 97 131 984 128

PO Box 448, South Morang Victoria 3752 Australia

Telephone: +61 3 9404 5579

info@thinkpublishing.com.au

www.thinkpublishing.com.au

Graphic Design:

Tristan Wilson

Jonathan Takle

Houses for Small Spaces

ISBN 978-0-9808314-8-1

Edited By:

Gary Takle

Contributors:

Emma Peacock

Jade de Souza

Corey Thomas

Business Development Manager:

Dom Shorthouse